What People Are Saying About . . .
Teens 911

"Reading Deborah Morris's adventures is more fun than a roller-coaster!"

—**Neil Shulman, M.D.**
author, *Doc Hollywood*

"Each of these stories would make exciting fiction, but to know that these events happened to real teens makes them jump off the page. No one can predict when he or she will be called on to be a hero, but these kids, called under the most trying circumstances, all proved themselves heroes."

—**Janice Williams**
KVET-FM (Austin)

"Wow! these stories do more than just tell true tales. They teach. They inspire. They motivate. They reveal the true character of youth—a character that is hidden until life-or-death choices must be made in a matter of seconds. Their lives are changed after living it, as will yours be after reading it."

—**Harry Hall**
syndicated columnist
C&S Media

Helicopter Crash and Other True Survival Stories

DEBORAH MORRIS

Health Communications, Inc.
Deerfield Beach, Florida

www.hci-online.com

Library of Congress Cataloging-in-Publication Data

Morris, Deborah.
   Teens 911 : snowbound, helicopter crash and other true survival
stories / Deborah Morris.
     p. cm.
   Summary: Fictionalized accounts of true incidents from across the
United States in which teenagers used their knowledge and skills to save
their own or someone else's life. Each story is followed by a quiz about
emergency procedures.
   Contents: Snowbound—Helicopter crash—River of no return—
Flameproof—Race to the finish.
   ISBN 0-7573-0039-1
   [1. Lifesaving—Fiction.   2. Heroes—Fiction.   3. Assistance in
emergencies—Fiction. 4.Courage—Fiction.]   I. Title.

PZ7.M82757 Te 2002
[Fic]—dc21

                                     2002068787

Publisher: Health Communications, Inc.
          3201 S.W. 15th Street
          Deerfield Beach, Florida 33442-8190

Cover illustration and design by Larissa Hise Henoch
Inside book formatting by Dawn Von Strolley Grove

CONTENTS

Snowbound

Justin and Aaron and their friend Van are lost in a howling storm. Can their faith and friendship get them through?

Staying awake in freshman English class at Mead High School was always a challenge, but Fridays were the worst. Aaron Peterson propped his chin on his hand and tried to keep his eyes open, but his mind kept drifting to the weekend ahead. Freedom was so close!

Aaron was a lean and athletic fifteen-year-old with dark hair and eyes. He stretched, flexing his muscles in case any of the girls were watching, but none of them seemed to notice. He sighed and hunched back over his desk.

When the bell finally rang, he walked out of class with his best friend, Justin Haeger, who was shorter than Aaron and had spiky, blond-tipped hair. Justin yawned, trying to shake off the stupefying effects of English.

"Hey Aaron, you want to spend the night over at my house? It's nice outside, and we can work on the fort." Nice days weren't to be wasted in Spokane, Washington, where rain and snow were the norm.

"Sounds good. Do you need to ask your parents first or anything?"

"Are you kidding? They won't mind. My mom and dad like you better than me!"

Aaron grinned. "Everybody likes me better than you, Justin. That's something you just need to accept." He dodged Justin's playful jab and waved to his friend before heading for his next class.

It was around three-thirty by the time he got to Justin's house. Karen Haeger greeted him casually. "I think Justin's out in the garage getting some nails and wood together. How's the latest fort coming along?"

"Slow," Aaron answered honestly. "But this one's easier since it's on the ground." He joined Justin in the garage and helped sort through the wood scraps. Justin's dad took woodworking jobs on the side, so there was usually a good selection.

"I think we've got enough of the right size," Aaron said, eyeing the stack. "If I'm riding on the back of your bike, I can't carry any six-foot boards."

"My mom wants us back by seven or eight, so we can't camp out this time."

Aaron shrugged. "Whatever. Let's just go."

Justin backed out his Kawasaki 100 and kick-started it, then Aaron climbed onto the back. Between his armful of wood and Justin's backpack, there wasn't much room. It's a good thing we're only going a mile or two, he thought as he settled onto the hard, narrow seat. The trail bike got them there faster than walking, but it was a very bumpy ride. The small engine sounded like an angry wasp.

The woods behind Justin's house were dense and over-grown. Justin skillfully wove through the trees until they were deep inside, hidden from all roads and trails. He pulled into the small, open area they'd picked for their latest fort and killed the engine. The sudden silence added to the feeling that they'd traveled miles from civilization.

The half-built fort was still there. Aaron tossed down the wood he'd brought and studied the odd-looking structure. "I think we should finish that wall and put on the roof. That way we can at least have a dry spot to sleep next time we camp out."

For the next hour they hammered and nailed, erecting a somewhat shaky wall and covering the top with several wide planks they'd brought out on another day. They left an opening in one wall that they could use as a door.

"What do you think?" Aaron asked, stepping back.

"Looks good to me. Let's quit now and build a fire."

Even when they didn't plan to stay overnight, they liked to build a fire. It added to the adventure of being alone in the woods, two men against the elements. They quickly gathered enough twigs and leaves to get a small fire started, then fed in a couple of larger sticks. Their goal was always to build the biggest fire possible without actually starting a forest fire. They got a nice blaze going and sat next to it as the woods slowly turned black around them.

Life was good.

"Did you bring anything to eat?" Aaron finally asked, half drowsy from the fire.

"No. Want to go hunting? Maybe we can catch a squirrel or something." Justin had gone on his first hunting trip with his dad when he was eighteen months old. He was a good hunter and tracker.

Aaron wrinkled his nose. "No way. Last time we ate a squirrel it tasted gross."

"Yeah, it was pretty bad. Maybe we could try for a moose next time."

"Uh-huh."

They sat quietly for a few minutes as the fire crackled and sparked. In the distance a coyote howled, a long and wavering cry.

Justin finally said, "We'd better start back. It's getting late." They used their water bottles to put out the fire and kicked dirt over it for good measure.

Another coyote howled, this time much closer. Aaron pulled out a flashlight and sent it around the woods, half-expecting it to pick up shining red eyes. The trees cast strange shadows in the harsh beam, but no eyes.

"Look! What's that?" Justin exclaimed, pointing. When Aaron spun around and aimed the flashlight in that direction, Justin snickered, "Oh sorry, thought I saw a cougar."

Aaron clicked off the flashlight. "You're sick, you know that?"

"Yeah."

Aaron waited until Justin had the Kawasaki started, then

climbed on behind him. It was a lot less crowded without the wood.

A few minutes later they were back at Justin's house. His dad's Ford pickup was in the driveway. They went in through the garage. Mr. and Mrs. Haeger were watching TV in the family room and looked up as the boys tramped in.

"There you are! I was starting to wonder," Mrs. Haeger said. "Do you guys want warmed-up lasagna or grilled cheese sandwiches with tomato soup?"

"Lasagna!" they answered in unison. They'd worked up an appetite building the fort.

"Did you see any interesting wildlife out there today?" asked Mr. Haeger.

Justin laughed. "Aaron thought he saw a cougar, but I didn't see anything."

"Justin pointed behind me and said, 'What's that?' I fell for it." He rolled his eyes.

Mr. Haeger smiled. "So where exactly did you go today?"

While Justin described the route they took to the newest fort, Aaron wandered into the kitchen. The lasagna smelled great, and he was starving.

Mrs. Haeger set plates and silverware on the breakfast bar. "So Aaron, how's your mom doing? I haven't talked with her in a while."

"She's okay." He watched as she slid two huge squares of steaming lasagna onto the plates. "Thanks, this looks great. Hey Justin! Food."

The boys sat side by side at the breakfast bar and wolfed down the lasagna. "This is a whole lot better than squirrel," Aaron whispered.

Justin grinned. "No joke. That was bad, like eating a rat."

"I'd have to be starving to death before I tried that again," Aaron said, "and I don't plan to ever get that hungry."

Into the Cold

The sky was a solid dirty white and the ground covered with snow as Aaron packed his skis and other gear for the weekend. Justin had invited him to come along on a church youth-group trip to Schweitzer Mountain Ski Resort in Idaho. Since they'd be leaving early in the morning, Aaron was going to spend the night at Justin's house and leave from there.

"Have fun!" his mom called out as he left. "I love you!"

Aaron replied automatically, "Yeah, you too. See you tomorrow!"

At Justin's house, preparations for the weekend ski trip were already in full force. About twenty-five kids would be going, and Mr. Haeger was one of the parent chaperones. He let Aaron in and said, "Justin and Van are playing video games. You can go on down."

Justin's room was in the basement of the split-level, ranch-style house. Van was another friend from school who liked to snowboard. He'd also be spending the night and going to Schweitzer Mountain. It was going to be an incredible trip!

Aaron stepped out into the garage long enough to lean his skis against the wall, then trotted downstairs. "Hey, what's up?" he greeted them.

Justin and Van were intent on their game. "Nothing much," Justin said over his shoulder. Van waved without turning. Aaron sat on the bed and watched until they tossed down the controllers.

Van stood up and stretched. He was shorter than Justin and Aaron, with curly brown hair. "So are you ready for this weekend? They're saying it's supposed to snow in the morning. We should have fresh powder."

Aaron grinned. "We'll be able to pull some sick tricks if we have a couple feet. I'd like to find a slope with untouched powder, before anybody else gets there. I can't wait!"

"Maybe we can find someplace where we can build a ramp without getting caught," Justin suggested. He and Van were snowboarders, and like skateboarders, they used ramps for tricks. Since ski resorts frowned on people building snow ramps, they'd have to keep it out of sight.

They stayed up late, talking excitedly about various tricks they planned to try. It was after 2 A.M. when they fell asleep.

The wake-up call at 6 A.M. came way too early. Mr. Haeger was already up and dressed. Justin, Aaron and Van were dragging as they pulled on ski pants, T-shirts, sweatshirts and wool socks. Aaron had debated about packing thermal underwear, but skiing always ended up being a workout. Once he got moving on the slopes, he'd be plenty warm enough in a T-shirt and sweats.

They tramped upstairs only half-awake, carrying their backpacks. Mr. Haeger told Justin in a quiet voice, "Let's get all the skis and boards out to the truck. Don't forget the lunches your mom made for us. We'll have worked up an appetite by lunchtime!"

"I'm ready for food now," Justin grumbled. "Are we going to get something to eat on the way?"

"We'll probably stop for gas and let everybody get out and buy snacks then. We don't have time now. We're supposed to leave the church at seven."

Aaron glanced out a window and gave a muted cheer. "Man, it's dumping snow out there! Look at this!" The others crowded around and peered out at the solid curtain of falling snow. The slopes would be perfect.

It was a quarter to seven when they pulled into the church parking lot. People were already loading their equipment into the two church vans. Brad, the youth group leader, was trotting back and forth, keeping things moving.

Aaron, Justin and Van jumped out at soon as Mr. Haeger parked. The frigid air quickly snapped them to full alertness. They laughed and joked as they trekked across the icy parking lot, squinting against the snow and puffing small white clouds into the air as they talked.

"I hear Schweitzer Mountain is premier," Aaron said. "It

has a high-speed quad lift and everything. I can't wait to get up there and rip!"

Justin was wearing a tan and red jacket with a knit cap and red mittens. He grinned. "Are we still gonna build a ramp?"

"Why not?" Van asked. "If we get caught we can just bust it up."

Their van was buzzing with excitement by the time they pulled out at seven o'clock. When they made a brief gas stop, Aaron, Justin and Van dashed inside and bought donuts. Lunch was going to be a long time away.

Schweitzer Mountain

Snow was still pouring from the sky when they reached the resort, and excitement among the teens rose to a fever pitch. This had to be a record snowfall, perfect for a day on the slopes.

"This is driving me insane!" Aaron exclaimed, staring longingly out the window. "I want to get out there!"

As soon as the van rolled to a stop, the boys grabbed their skis, snowboards and goggles and jumped out. They decided to drop their lunches off at the lodge. They didn't want to worry about squashing or losing them.

Mr. Haeger smiled and waved as the three struck off purposefully toward the lifts. "Have fun, boys! In case I miss you at lunch, don't forget to meet back here at four o'clock."

"Okay!" they replied. They were in a hurry to get up the mountain and make some runs while the powder was fresh. They reached the lift and settled side by side in the seat, the three of them easily fitting into the quad lift. It swept them up the mountainside at a brisk fifteen or twenty miles per hour. Between the wind and the blowing snow, they were all chilled by the time they reached the top and jumped off.

"So where do you want to start?" Justin asked, stamping his feet. There were a number of different trails to choose from, but in the swirling whiteness they couldn't see more than twenty feet in any direction. The trails were clearly marked with snowlines, though—poles wrapped in eye-catching neon tape and marked with small flags. Everyone knew better than to go out of bounds.

"Let's work our way around to the backside of the mountain," Aaron suggested, using the back of a glove to clear snow from his goggles. "There'll be fewer people skiing there."

"Okay."

Aaron led off, since skis gave him more speed and con-trol over direction and turns. Justin and Van followed on their snowboards, enjoying the more free-wheeling feel-ing of sliding down the mountainside. They angled to their right, happily skiing and boarding through the fresh powder. Aaron stopped now and then to let the others catch up.

After a short run, they spotted another chairlift and decided to take it up. It would get them farther away from the crowded trails near the main quad lift and put them closer to the back slope of the mountain.

Once they got off at the top, they looked around to

decide which trail to take from there. The snow was blowing almost horizontal, making it hard to see the signs. They finally settled on a wide, smooth trail that looked interesting. The powder was fresh and unmarked, exactly what they'd hoped for. Aaron pushed off with Justin and Van close on his heels.

They made several short runs, then Justin waved and pointed to the far right of the trail. "Let's stop and build our ramp over there. The trees will help hide it."

They made their way across the trail and set to work, gathering up the fine, powdery snow and packing it into a solid mound. They were all sweating by the time they had a usable kicker ramp, a launch ramp made of snow.

Aaron in flight.

Photo Credit: Brian Plonka

Aaron stepped back and looked at it doubtfully. "You think it'll stay together? This dry snow is hard to pack."

"Only one way to find out," Justin said with a grin.

He led off with a back flip, hitting the jump just right and throwing his head back as soon as he got air. His feet and board shot up and over his head in a complete circle, coming level again just in time for him to land and continue riding forward. It was perfect. Aaron and Van clapped and cheered.

"I'm the best!" Justin said modestly, raising his hands in the air. "Yes!"

For the next half-hour they took turns making runs. Justin attempted some 720s—two complete 360-degree rotations in mid-air, which were supposed to be landed riding forward—but he usually ended up face down in the snow. After that, he stuck with back flips and rodeo flips—back flips done sideways. He landed most of those.

They used the ramp until it fell apart, then decided to continue down the slope. Aaron once again led off, following the cleared trail that angled slightly to the left.

The wind was picking up, making it more and more difficult to see through the blowing snow. Even the brightly colored trail markers were hard to spot. The boys knew

Justin and Aaron practicing tricks.

Photo Credit: Brian Plonka

other people were skiing all over the mountain, maybe even on the same run, but as they skied on into the whiteness they saw no one else.

The snow continued to fall, quickly filling in the tracks behind them.

Without a Trace

Aaron stood alone, his back to the wind as he waited for Justin and Van to catch up. They had been skiing for over an hour, probably covering six miles. For the past half-hour, they hadn't seen any trail markers. They were also getting into more trees.

When Justin and Van swooshed into sight on their boards, Aaron motioned them over. "Look guys, I'm still not seeing any trail markers. Have either of you seen one?"

The other boys shook their heads. Justin said, "There's got to be a couple feet of new powder on top of the snow base. Maybe the markers got buried!" Some of the poles were only four or five feet tall. A record snowfall *could* bury them. Many of the trees were half-buried, their trunks and lower branches completely covered.

Aaron wiped his goggles. "Shouldn't we have run into the main lift by now?"

"We probably just missed it," Justin said. "Snow is good at hiding sounds."

The three looked at each other. Intentionally jumping snowlines to ski out of bounds was a serious infraction, mainly because it was dangerous. The resort kept the trails clear, and the ski patrol made regular rounds, but once you went out of bounds you were on your own.

"Well, we can't go back up," Aaron said. "We'd have to wade through chest-deep snow for miles!" He glanced up at the snow still pouring from the sky.

"Let's cut across to the main road and hitch a ride back up to the lodge," Justin suggested. "We can't be too far from the road, and it'll be easier to go sideways than up." Aaron and Van quickly agreed.

It was only about ten o'clock. They set off in high spirits, sure they would make it back to the top in plenty of time for lunch.

They'd only gone a short way when the terrain suddenly flattened out and became so thick with trees that they could no longer ski or board. They needed at least some slope to keep up enough speed to skim across the snow's surface. They finally had to stop.

"This isn't working," said Aaron. "We're going to have to walk." He snapped off his skis and crossed them behind his head. Justin and Van slung their boards across their backs, holding them by their leashes. The snow came up to their hips.

Justin eyed the path ahead, using a gloved hand to shield his face from the snow flurries. "We can take turns breaking a trail. This isn't going to be much fun."

That turned out to be a huge understatement. They quickly discovered that it wasn't possible to kick or shove an open trail through the snow; it was as solid as a wall. The leader had to struggle for each step, raising his knee almost to his chest to get a foot on top of the snow, then shifting his weight forward to step down hard. It was only slightly easier for the other two since they still had to lift their legs high to step into the leader's packed-down footprints.

Aaron led for a stretch. After only fifty feet his clothes were soaked with sweat, and his breathing was labored. The air was thin at that altitude. He squinted ahead, hoping to see some sign of the road. He couldn't imagine going much farther like that. He was already exhausted.

They were struggling along, trying to ignore the burning in their muscles and lungs, when the feathery snowfall turned to freezing rain. It pelted their faces with stinging ice chips. They hunched over, trying to shield their faces as they slogged on.

This is a nightmare, Aaron thought. Lunchtime had come and gone, but he doubted anybody would worry that they hadn't shown up. Justin's dad would probably think they were having so much fun that they hadn't wanted to stop to eat.

"I'm hungry," he said aloud to get his mind off their situation. "Either of you guys bring a picnic basket?"

Justin answered breathlessly, "No, and I can't even catch a squirrel in this snow. I can make you a great deal on a snow sandwich, though."

"Thanks a lot," Aaron said sarcastically. He was hot and thirsty, which seemed ironic considering that they were practically buried in frozen water. He grabbed a handful of snow and popped it into his mouth, letting it melt and trickle down his throat. It only seemed to make a few drops of water. He ate handful after handful but was still thirsty.

"So are we there yet?" Justin asked jokingly. He glanced back at Van, who had grown very quiet. "Hey Van! You doing okay?"

"Yeah," Van answered shortly.

"That's good. I'm pretty sure we're almost there." Justin knew Van had much less experience in the outdoors than he or Aaron. He didn't want him to get discouraged.

Aaron chimed in. "Hang in there, Van. Every step gets us that much closer to the road."

On top of stinging their faces, the freezing rain formed a hard crust on the snow's surface that made breaking the trail even harder. Now whenever Aaron lifted his heavy boot and planted it on top of the snow, it would bear his weight until he pulled himself almost all the way up—then the crust would give and his forward step would punch down through the snow, ending in a jarring impact three feet down. It was exhausting, like climbing a giant staircase.

Justin was leading when he suddenly stopped and looked around. "Hey guys," he said. "I think we're in some kind of valley."

Aaron and Van peered around, noting the slopes on both sides. Between the freezing rain and their own exertions, their clothes were sodden. The bitterly cold breeze that swept through the valley left them all shivering.

"We can't stand still in this wind," Aaron said through numb lips. "Let's try to work our way up to a peak and see if we can figure out exactly where we are."

It took almost superhuman effort for the three to fight through the deepening snowdrifts to a small ridge. The only thing that kept them going was the hope that they'd get to the top and see the road directly ahead. They could picture it in their minds—the road snaking up the mountain only a short downhill slope away, traveled by lots of cars heading up to the lodge.

Aaron didn't realize how much he was counting on it until they stumbled the last few feet to the top and looked down. There was no road, no cars . . . just deep snow and trees in every direction.

"Oh man," he whispered, a hard knot forming in his gut. They were lost, and in another few hours the sun would be going down.

Hidden Dangers

The shock of discovering they were still far from help left the three teens speechless for a moment, but the cold wind quickly whipped them back into motion. The only good thing about their new position was that they were on a downhill slope. They strapped on their skis and boards.

Aaron led off, grateful to be speeding across the snow for a while instead of slogging through it. Despite being cold, hungry and exhausted, he felt his spirits lift. They weren't beaten yet! The road had to be somewhere ahead, and he was determined to find it.

He was almost upon the crevasse before he saw it. A hidden stream had made a deep cut in the snow three feet across and ten feet deep. With a startled exclamation, he veered around it, then yelled back a warning, "Look out!"

Almost before he finished yelling, he heard a panicked shout and turned back. Snowboards were less maneuverable than skis, and Van hadn't been able to turn in time.

He had gone over the edge.

"Van!" Falling into the stream could easily be fatal, even if Van hadn't hit the frigid water. The crevasse was deep, and they had no rope. There'd be no way to pull him out if he was at the bottom.

"Aaron! Help!" Van's voice was high-pitched with fear. Aaron skied as close as he dared to the edge, then popped off his skis and inched even closer. He peered over the side to find Van "punched in" just a few feet down, both arms wedged into the snow wall. Somehow he'd had the presence of mind to halt his fall in the only way possible. His board, still attached to his feet, was also partially punched into the snow.

"I'm right here, man! I'll get you out." Knowing he needed firm footing, Aaron stomped his heavy boots until both legs were punched deep into the snow before leaning down to reach for Van. He grabbed one of Van's wrists and tugged with all his strength. Van used his other arm to help as much as he could, but both of them were scared and out of breath by the time Van slid onto the surface.

Aaron slumped back into the snow like it was a recliner. "Well," he said, almost giddy with relief. "I guess you're okay now."

Van tried to laugh. "Yeah, I almost fell right into the water! Can you believe that?"

"I hope you're not planning to do that again because next time I might just leave you there." He smiled to show he was kidding. Neither of them wanted to think about how close Van had come to death. Things like that weren't supposed to happen to fifteen-year-olds.

Their slightly hysterical conversation was interrupted by a distant scream. It snapped them to attention, and they both scrambled to their feet.

"Where's Justin?" asked Van. "He was right behind me." Between the blowing snow and the trees it was hard to tell from which direction the sound was coming.

Aaron spoke quickly. "I'll go find him. You stay here."

"Forget that! I'm coming, too."

Together they floundered through the snow, following Justin's muffled shouts. They found him partway down a tree well, a deep snow shaft that ran straight down along the trunk of a half-buried tree. Snow wells were notorious death traps, often collapsing on top of skiers and suffocating them. Justin was clinging precariously to an icy branch, dangling over a nine- or ten-foot drop down an extremely narrow shaft. If he fell the rest of the way he'd be wedged in by the hard-packed snow and too far down to reach.

"Hang on! We'll get you out," Aaron yelled. He and Van threw themselves flat and grabbed Justin's arms, wriggling backwards to haul him up and out. As soon as he reached the surface they all scrambled away from the shaft.

"Thanks," Justin said weakly. "I never even saw it until I started falling."

Two near-fatal accidents in a matter of minutes had left them all shaken. "Well, I guess that made things a little more adventurous," Aaron finally said in an attempt to lighten things up.

"Right," Justin replied. "Just another chapter in the story of our lives."

Aaron forced a smile. "Yeah, it might be the last one, but at least it'll be exciting! Come on, we'd better get moving. It's starting to get dark. We need to hurry up and find that road."

Nighttime came early in the winter. It was already past four o'clock, the time the church group had been scheduled to leave for home. At this moment, they should have been sitting shoulder to shoulder in a warm van, laughing about the day's adventures. Instead they were staggering, exhausted and shivering, through hip-deep snow.

@   @   @

Ron Haeger glanced impatiently at his watch, then squinted up toward the slopes, still obscured by the falling snow. They had been waiting almost a half-hour for Justin, Aaron and Van to show up in the parking lot. All the other kids had their gear in the vans and were ready to go.

"The boys aren't usually this irresponsible," he told Brad, the youth leader, apologetically. "Listen, why don't you guys go ahead? I don't want to hold everybody else up."

"I'll stay with you," Brad offered. "Let me go tell the others."

They waved as the vans pulled out, then turned their attention back to the mountain.

As of yet, nobody had discovered the three unclaimed lunches still sitting in the lodge.

Fading Daylight

Aaron flexed his numb fingers inside his damp and ice-encrusted gloves and tried not to think about holding a cup of hot chocolate. Even if he didn't get to drink it, he'd like to warm his hands around it.

He ate some more snow instead.

"I think I just saw Bigfoot," Justin announced casually, interrupting Aaron's gloomy thoughts.

"Good. Maybe we can use his phone."

"And weren't there some escaped criminals out here awhile back? They're probably stalking us, too."

Aaron smiled through cracked lips. "Then they're pretty dumb criminals. We don't have anything. It would make better sense for *us* to stalk *them*!"

Van joined in and told jokes for a while, but as the light faded and the temperature dropped, he grew silent and lagged farther and farther behind. Finally he stopped.

"Hey guys, can we take a break?" he asked. His face was pinched with cold and his feet were dragging. "I'm tired."

Aaron shook his head. "We'll freeze if we stop moving. C'mon, we're all tired. You can do this."

"Why don't we make a snow cave? That way we can get out of the wind and have someplace to sleep. It's almost dark."

"No way!" Aaron retorted. "You're crazy if you think I'm going to spend the night on this mountain. Besides, I'm starving. No way are we going to stop."

Van shook his head wearily but kept walking. Justin gave his shoulder a friendly punch. "Look, let's just make the best of it. It can't be much farther."

Even to himself, the words didn't sound convincing.

@   @   @

The last chairlift for the day brought the last group of skiers down off the mountain. Justin, Aaron and Van weren't among them.

Ron Haeger looked over at Brad. "Something's wrong," he said quietly. "I'm going to the ski patrol office."

The sky overhead was already turning dim.

Fade to Black

Daylight had dissolved into a gray world of swirling snow. The three boys walked on like automatons, too tired and cold to joke anymore. Aaron was leading again, straining his eyes in the fading light for any sign of the road.

By now their families must know they were missing. Were searchers out on the mountain looking for them? If so, they were probably looking in the wrong places. They had no way of knowing they had wandered out of bounds.

Aaron shook off the depressing thought. He was most

concerned about Van. He kept falling back and complaining of being sleepy, one of the first signs of hypothermia. Aaron and Justin kept him going with a combination of encouragement and teasing.

"Hey, look at that cougar track!" Justin exclaimed, pointing to a nearly indistinguishable dent in the snow. "Better keep up with us, Van, or the cougars will eat you. They always pick off the stragglers first." Aaron gave him a questioning look, but Van stuck closer for a while.

They walked until it was pitch black, then they walked some more. As the temperature continued to drop, it became clear that Van was in trouble. His eyes were dull, and he was taking longer and longer to respond when they talked to him.

"I think Van's losing it," Justin told Aaron through chattering teeth. "He looks like a zombie. We have to do something."

They finally stopped, not only because of Van's condition but because they kept stumbling in the dark over fallen logs and other obstacles. In those conditions, a broken leg could be a fatal injury.

Aaron waited for Van to catch up. "We're going to find somewhere to dig your snow cave now. Just hang in there a little longer, okay?" Van didn't answer.

Aaron and Justin had made many snow caves at home after plows had cleared the streets, so they knew what to look for. They stopped when they found a huge tree with a good build-up of snow at its base.

"Come help us, Van," Justin called. "The faster we get it

done the faster we can all get inside and try to warm up."
Van's eyes looked glazed, and he mumbled something but
didn't move. Justin didn't have the energy to persuade
him. He turned away and went to help Aaron.

Now that they had stopped walking and generating
heat, their sweaty and rain-soaked clothes quickly
became stiff with ice. The wind was biting. Within minutes they were shivering so hard they could barely talk.
Their hands felt like frozen clubs as they scraped snow
away from the center of the drift.

I wonder if I'm going to lose my fingers, Aaron thought
almost clinically as he packed snow to form thick walls.
He felt himself slowing down, getting clumsy and sleepy,
but he had no choice. If they didn't build a shelter from
the wind they'd all freeze to death.

Justin was also slowing down. "My fingers hurt," he
mumbled, then seemed surprised that he had spoken
aloud. Aaron looked at him worriedly. Without Justin's
help he didn't think he could finish the shelter.

Please help us, God, he prayed wearily. *We're in
trouble here. Help us get this done.*

Despite waging a losing battle against the cold, they
finally finished the snow cave—a rectangle with four-foot
tall walls to block the wind, and a half-roof formed by
their snowboards and skis. They crawled in and huddled
close together, their upper bodies sheltered by the clumsy
roof.

This is like lying in a snow coffin, thought Aaron as he
flung an arm around Van's shoulders to warm him. He

wasn't concerned about "personal space" or what anyone else might think. The only thing that concerned him now was survival.

Somehow they had to last out the night.

@ @ @

Ron Haeger watched numbly as the last hint of daylight disappeared from the sky. There was no chance, no chance at all, that the boys could be found in the vast and inky darkness. They might as well have been lost on the moon.

He prayed for their safety, then added under his breath, "Hang on, Justin. Dig in and hang on until we can get to you."

Waking Nightmares

Justin gasped when the truck pulled up and stopped outside their snow cave. "They've found us!" he said excitedly, straining to sit up. "Look!"

He was angry when Aaron responded by shaking him roughly and yelling: "Snap out of it, Justin! You're seeing things again. You need to wake up."

Justin blinked in confusion, and the truck disappeared. He felt like crying. "*This* is a nightmare," he whispered. "I don't want to wake up. Leave me alone."

"No! Move around or you're going to freeze." Aaron's voice was harsh and cracked. For hours he had kept himself awake by thinking about his family and praying. His body was shaking so hard he felt like he was having convulsions. He had removed his gloves, which were soaked through and frozen solid.

Justin and Van had drifted in and out of consciousness, occasionally babbling about needing to do homework or going to the hot tub outside. Every ten or fifteen minutes Aaron shook them awake and made them answer him. He felt bad dragging them back from pleasant dreams of warmth and home, but he was afraid not to. With hypothermia, it was all too easy to drift off to sleep and never wake up.

"Van! Are you awake?" he asked sharply.

Van jumped like he'd been shocked. "Yeah," he answered. "Where are we?"

"Still on the mountain. Try to stay awake, okay?"

"Yeah." An instant later he was asleep again.

Aaron was overwhelmed with despair. How long could he keep this up? Dawn was still hours away. He lay back to rest for just a minute, images of his parents' grief-stricken faces flitting across his mind. I feel so bad for them, he thought groggily. This is going to be so hard on them.

He drifted away.

Sometime later he awoke in confusion. Somebody was shaking him so hard that his arms and legs were flopping around like a rag doll's. It took a tremendous effort for him to open his eyes. He was puzzled when he finally managed to crack his eyes to find that nobody was there.

Aaron stared up into the darkness trying to figure out

where he was and why his arms and legs were flopping around by themselves. When he finally recognized his surroundings a stab of pure fear jolted him fully awake. He'd fallen asleep!

He stared down, horrified to realize he couldn't control the violent spasms wracking his body. Icy pain ripped through his body as his legs drummed helplessly against the packed snow. With jerky movements he hauled himself up to a sitting position. "P-Please," he stammered through frozen lips, a strangled prayer for help.

It seemed to take forever, but the wild flailings of his limbs eventually slowed down. He leaned over Justin and shoved him roughly. "Hey Justin, wake up! Come on, man, open your eyes!"

He was relieved when Justin groaned. In the dark, he couldn't tell if either of his friends were breathing.

"What?" Justin demanded hoarsely.

"Sit up for a minute and move around," Aaron said. "Come on, just do it!"

Justin rolled clumsily to one side and pushed himself up. "There, you happy? Don't wake me up anymore. I was dreaming I was at home under my sheets." He was shivering so hard that his teeth kept banging together. His arms and legs were also shaking uncontrollably.

"I'm going to keep waking you up, so get over it. Help me get Van up."

Together they shook Van and yelled until he answered. It took Aaron a moment to realize that there was something different about Van.

He was no longer shivering.

The thought sank into Aaron's brain with molasses-like slowness. There was something about not shivering in the cold, something bad. If he could only remember. . . .

Hypothermia.

Shivering was the body's natural response to extreme cold; the muscle spasms actually generated body heat. When somebody suddenly stopped shivering in the cold it was often because they'd moved into a critical state of hypothermia.

They were losing Van.

Aaron was determined to stay awake and keep Van alive, no matter what it took. He sat hunched in the snow cave, arms wrapped around his knees, rocking back and forth in the frigid air.

I wish I'd said more to my mom when I left, he thought, remembering his casual "me, too" response when she'd called out that she loved him. If he didn't make it back home, those would be the last words she'd hear from him. He swallowed painfully.

God, help me stay awake, he prayed silently. *And help me make it back home to my family. Help all of us make it back home.*

Sometime during the long night the snow tapered off and the wind died down. In the stillness, Aaron heard a faint train whistle. It raised his hopes. If there was a train within hearing distance they couldn't be that far from civilization!

Come on, he silently urged the dawn. Waiting for

sunrise, he felt like a vampire waiting for night to come. As soon as it was light enough to see they'd emerge from their snow coffin and start walking again.

Dawn, when it finally came, was a subtle shift from black to gray. It took Aaron a few minutes to realize that he could make out the shapes of the trees outside. He shifted painfully to his knees and started shaking Justin and Van.

It was time to go.

Last Chance

Justin couldn't stand up. "I think my leg is frozen solid, Aaron," he said in a voice tight with fear. "It's like a rock. I can't feel my toes at all."

Aaron was stunned. If Justin couldn't walk, there was no way they'd be able to reach help. They were all weak from hunger and exhaustion. Van was standing, but too dazed to be much help.

"You've got to walk, Justin. It's probably just numb from the cold. Keep trying to move it."

As Justin worked desperately to knead life back into his leg, Aaron took stock of their situation. The weather was better, with no freezing rain or wind gusts, and the first few streaks of sunrise were already glinting in the sky. They should be able to make better time and see where they were going.

If they were going. If Justin couldn't walk, Aaron wasn't going to leave him. They'd just have to wait and pray that the ski patrol would find them in time.

Justin was still pounding on his leg. "It feels like a dead stump, but I can bend my knee a little now. Maybe if I can get my circulation going it'll be able to bear my weight."

"Good," Aaron said with relief. He looked down at his bare hands, then glanced at the skis and boards still covering the snow cave. "I think we should ditch our stuff. It's too much work to lug it all along with us when we can't use it."

Justin nodded. He had also discarded his frozen gloves during the night. He flexed his knee gingerly and said, "I'm going to try again to stand up." The first time he put a little weight on his leg it buckled under him, but after several more attempts it held.

"Let's go," he said. "Just take it slow until I get some feeling back."

Since Aaron was in the best shape of the three he led the way, but it scared him to be the one responsible for picking the direction. What if he led them farther into the wilderness?

Show me the way out, he prayed. *Please guide me!*

In the distance a train whistle suddenly wailed. Aaron's eyes widened as he tried to locate the sound. Train tracks, like rivers and streams, often lead to civilization. He determined to follow the whistle as best he could.

They followed several snow-covered logging roads that looked like they were angling in the right direction, but none of them went far. Aaron, walking some distance ahead, finally stopped to let Justin and Van catch up.

"Do you see anything?" Justin asked hopefully as he

limped up. The sensation had returned in his leg, bringing with it painful muscle cramps.

Aaron shook his head. "Not yet."

Justin glanced up at the overcast sky. "I hope we're not going to keep walking all the way into Canada," he said tiredly. They weren't that far from the border.

It had been a full day since they ate the donuts they'd bought on the way to the resort. It seemed an eternity.

The hours that followed passed slowly. Too exhausted to joke or even talk, the three struggled on through the snow in gloomy silence. Their throats remained parched despite handfuls of snow, and their empty stomachs were knotted with both cold and hunger. They were nearing the end of their strength.

Aaron felt increasingly nailed by guilt. His friends were depending on him, but if he was leading in the right direction, shouldn't they have reached the road by now? Each time he stopped to rest, he dreaded the question from Justin and Van: "Do you see anything?" It killed him to watch their faces drop each time he had to answer: "No."

Finally he couldn't take it anymore. He was several minutes ahead of the others when he reached a small clearing. He stopped, unsure about which way to go from there. Every direction looked the same! As he hesitated, knowing that the wrong choice could cost all of them their lives, despair swept over him like an avalanche. For the first time since he was five years old he burst into tears.

"Oh God, we're going to die!" he sobbed. "Please help me choose the right direction!" He sank to his knees and leaned forward till his face was buried in the snow, muffling his sobs.

Any other time he would have felt stupid crying his eyes out with his head shoved into the snow, but now a deep sense of peace slowly stole over him. He sat quietly for a moment, then stood up and wiped his face. By the time Justin and Van reached the clearing he had picked a direction.

Five minutes later he came to a ridge and looked down to see an unnaturally straight line running across the tangled landscape. He stared, then let out a jubilant yell as he saw several tiny cars moving past.

"I found it!" he shouted. "Van! Justin! It's the road!"

Still Seeking Refuge

Justin had a hard time making out the words, but there was no mistaking Aaron's excitement. He said, "Come on, Van!" and started running.

The three boys tumbled joyfully down the hill, no longer feeling the cold. They crunched over fresh snowmobile tracks crisscrossed in the snow and ran on till they reached the railroad tracks where the train's whistle had called to them.

It was celebration time.

They started waving and yelling before they even reached the highway, but the passing cars didn't slow down. Even when they ran onto the shoulder of the road and tried frantically to flag down a car, the driver passed after only the briefest glance.

The same thing happened with the next car. And the next.

"I can't believe this!" Justin exclaimed in frustration. "They aren't going to stop!"

Aaron looked resigned. "These people are going to feel so bad when they hear about us."

"So what do we do now?"

"Keep walking."

They came to a house a few minutes later and knocked on the door, wondering what they should say if someone answered. When a man finally came to the door, Justin said awkwardly, "Uh, we're the kids that are lost."

"I know!" the man said unexpectedly. "It's been all over the news. Come in and get warm!"

After over twenty-four hours of endless cold, the warmth of the house was almost painful. The man motioned for the boys to sit down. "My name's Bill Findley. Let me get those frozen boots off your feet, then I'll call an ambulance. You boys need to go get checked out at the hospital."

Aaron wordlessly held out a boot. "Thanks," he said hoarsely. "I'm glad you were home. We couldn't get any of the cars to stop."

"The only reason I'm home today is because I'm recovering from a back injury. I'm a search and rescue volunteer who'd normally be out there looking for you. I never expected you to turn up at my door!"

The three teens looked at each other and smiled

Aaron, Justin and Ron Haeger at the mountain.

incredulously through cracked lips. "I guess we were really lucky," Justin said.

Aaron nodded, fumbling to unzip his jacket with frozen fingers. "I didn't feel very lucky while we were out there, but I'm starting to now. Mostly I feel hungry, though. Do you have anything we can eat?"

Mr. Findley shook his head regretfully. "You shouldn't eat anything until you get checked out. I'm calling the ambulance now, though, so they'll be here soon. You should be able to get something to eat at the hospital."

Aaron's face fell, but Justin shook his head. "Don't worry about him. He's *always* starving, even when he's frozen. He'll survive."

A few minutes later, the wail of an ambulance approaching on the highway marked the end of their ordeal.

Aaron, Justin and Van were treated for dehydration, frostbite and hypothermia and released the same day, although Aaron was disappointed that instead of the chili he requested when he first arrived at the hospital, they brought him some kind of vegetable soup.

They later learned that wind gusts of 50–70 mph had combined with an eighteen-inch snowfall to create

snowdrifts over ten feet high on Saturday, and that the temperature at the base of the resort registered twenty-three degrees overnight. The windchill on the mountainside probably dipped well below zero.

Van has since moved away, but Aaron and Justin still enjoy skiing and snowboarding.

Would You Know How to Survive . . . in Extreme Cold?

Take this quiz and find out!

1. _____ is as important as having basic needs like a sleeping bag.
   a. A signal mirror
   b. The will to survive
   c. A flashlight
   d. Clean underwear

2. **It's better to wear:**
   a. a single thick layer of clothing than several layers of lightweight clothing that add up to the same thickness
   b. several layers of lightweight clothing that add up to the same thickness as a single thick layer
   c. nylon instead of wool
   d. a stereo headset to keep your ears warm and your spirits up

3. _____ can make you lose body heat.
   a. Sweating
   b. Sitting directly on a cold rock or in the snow
   c. Breathing through your mouth
   d. All of the above

4. **You can lose 40–45 percent of your body heat if:**
   a. you take deep breaths without covering your mouth and nose
   b. you're not wearing gloves
   c. your jacket is partially unzipped
   d. your head isn't covered

5. **Shivering causes the body to:**
   a. produce heat
   b. become fatigued
   c. lose 10–15 degrees core temperature
   d. a and b

6. _____ **are some of the earliest warning signs of hypothermia.**
   a. Shivering, lack of coordination, personality change
   b. A cold nose, stinging eyes, intense thirst
   c. Hallucinations, loss of memory, unconsciousness
   d. Hiccups that won't go away

7. **To help you stay warm and prevent hypothermia, you should:**
   a. work up a sweat with your jacket tightly zipped
   b. curl up in a fetal position with your hands in your armpits
   c. dance and wiggle with your jacket partially unzipped so you don't sweat
   d. think of warm things like a fire or hot chocolate

8. **Eating snow will:**
   a. quench your thirst but make your teeth hurt

b. lower your core temperature and increase the risk of hypothermia

c. make you feel less hungry

d. make you sick to your stomach

9. **Severe signs of hypothermia requiring immediate action include:**

a. decrease in shivering

b. disorientation (becoming dazed or extremely confused)

c. becoming semiconscious and hard to wake

d. all of the above

10. **To prevent frostbite on your face, you should:**

a. stretch and wrinkle the skin by "making faces"

b. walk backwards into the wind when it's below freezing

c. slap yourself on the cheeks every 30–60 seconds

d. avoid licking your lips

11. **To treat frostbite on your hands, you should:**

a. rub snow on the frozen areas

b. place your hands under your armpits

c. clap your hands often

d. keep your hands elevated (raised) at regular intervals

12. **Make camp early so you:**

a. have plenty of time to build a shelter

b. have enough light to see what you're doing

c. aren't too tired to make an adequate shelter

d. all of the above

13. **Construct a shelter:**
    a. in a tree if possible to stay off the frozen ground
    b. larger than is needed so air can circulate
    c. just large enough to hold the people who'll be inside it
    d. by burrowing into a snow drift and letting your body heat melt a snow cave for you

14. **When exposed to extreme cold in a group, you should:**
    a. appoint an experienced member to watch for signs of hypothermia or frostbite
    b. adopt the survivor's attitude: "Every man for himself!"
    c. use your collective body heat in an emergency by removing your clothes and huddling together in a sleeping bag or enclosed shelter
    d. a and c

15. **The best way to prevent hypothermia is to:**
    a. prepare for the worst by wearing waterproof and windproof clothing
    b. carry water and high-energy or high-sugar snacks
    c. pay attention to your body's distress signals and respond quickly
    d. all of the above

Answers: 1-b, 2-b, 3-d, 4-d, 5-d, 6-a, 7-c, 8-b, 9-d, 10-a, 11-b, 12-d, 13-c, 14-d, 15-d

Give yourself five points for each correct answer, then check your score below:

70–75: *Teens 911 Top Gun.* You've demonstrated an unusually high level of knowledge and skills. Congratulations!

60–65: You've demonstrated an above-average level of knowledge and skills. Not bad.

50–55: While you've demonstrated at least some basic knowledge, it's not enough to keep you (or someone you're trying to help) out of trouble.

45 or Below: You should plan to stay indoors all winter, or plan to vacation in Florida or California, because you're definitely not ready to tackle extreme cold!

Helicopter Crash

Jodi Itri must save her father from a contraption she herself is scared of.

J odi!" Deputy Sheriff Don Itri walked through the small house, the silver star on his chest gleaming against his khaki uniform. Outside the night sky was clear, the air crisp with the first hint of fall. "Jodi, where are you at?"

Jodi Itri, thirteen, finally ran into the living room. "Sorry, Dad," she panted. "I was looking for my shoes."

Mr. Itri nodded, a grin lighting up his deeply tanned face, which was adorned with a bushy mustache. "You still sure you want to do this? Surveillance can be pretty boring, you know."

Jodi's eyes were bright as she replied, "Positive!" She often rode with her dad in his patrol car, but this was the first time he had allowed her to come along on a narcotics surveillance. It sounded exciting, especially since it would all take place late at night.

It was about nine-thirty in the small town of Fredericksburg, Texas. Mr. Itri and several other officers planned to set up night-vision binoculars about half a mile from a house in a part of Gillespie County where they suspected drug activity. All they'd do is watch the people who came and went. Jodi would be in no danger.

Not that I would mind a little danger, Jodi thought. Ever since school let out, she had been stuck at home. The most exciting thing she'd done all summer was go to the movies with her friend Skyla. She was ready for some action.

"So what are you going to do if you see people with drugs, Dad?" she asked eagerly as they crossed the yard to where the patrol car was parked. "Are you just going to sit there and watch, or are you going to arrest them?"

Her father laughed and said affectionately, "You're pretty bloodthirsty, Brat! No arrests tonight, I'm afraid. This is observation only." He nodded toward the car. "Now get in and put on your seat belt. And don't touch anything!"

The control panel in the patrol car had rows of buttons and switches. He'd explained what each did a million times, but Jodi always forgot. The only ones she remembered for sure were the siren and lights. Once, when she was riding with him at night, he'd let her turn them on for a few seconds. They'd cruised down a deserted back road under a full moon with the siren wailing and the blue and red lights flickering all around them. He was used to it, but she thought it looked cool.

It took about half an hour to reach the surveillance point. The four officers had decided to set up on a small hillside that looked down on the house they'd be watching. Once they got there, though, they had a hard time finding a spot that would give them a clear view through the trees. They had to see without being seen.

Jodi knew better than to interrupt, but once the night-vision binoculars were set up on the tripod she asked, "Can I look?"

Most of the police force had met Jodi and her big sister, Lisa. "Sure," said one of the officers. "It'll look funny to you, though. Night vision turns things green."

Jodi carefully placed her eyes to the lenses and took in the scene below. It was just a house, but through the binoculars, every detail sprang to life, bathed in a bright green glow. She could see the number on the mailbox and a weed growing in the yard. She lifted her face from the binoculars and peered down through the darkness, amazed at the difference. She could barely make out the outline of the house, much less the details.

She looked again. "Why does it turn everything green?" she asked, her eye to the lens.

"It helps your eyes stay adjusted so when you look away, you'll still be able to see okay in dim light. Keeps your eyes dilated."

Jodi thought for a moment. "But how do these work? I mean, how does it make things look bright even when it's completely dark outside?"

Mr. Itri stroked his mustache. "First of all, you're not really looking 'through' these binoculars like you would normal ones. What you're seeing is actually a screen, sort of a real little TV screen that shows the images with amplified light. Does that make sense?"

"No," Jodi answered honestly.

Don Itri looked to his fellow officers for help, but they just smiled. "Hm. Okay, you know there are some kinds of light, like infrared, that aren't visible to the human eye, right?"

"Right."

"Well, night vision can pick up light we can't see, like the near-infrared light that comes from the moon and stars. It uses energy from the power pack to intensify that light and display it on the little screen so we can see it. Then the eyepiece magnifies the image on the screen so everything looks bigger and closer, just like regular binoculars."

"Cool," Jodi said. She finally stepped back so the officers could start their surveillance.

As the moon slowly crossed the sky and midnight turned to one o'clock, Jodi sat quietly. Her dad had brought a thermos of coffee for himself and a thermos of hot chocolate for her, plus a couple honey buns to help keep them awake. Every now and then distant car lights would send the officers to the night-vision binoculars so they could note the time, take down license plate numbers and record descriptions of the people. In between, they let Jodi peek through the lenses a few more times.

By about 3 A.M., the stream of visitors had stopped and the house had grown quiet. Mr. Itri stood up and stretched his cramped muscles.

"Let's pack it in," he said tiredly. "Jodi, are you ready to go home?"

"I guess." She'd been yawning for a while, but she wasn't going to complain. She knew her father counted on her to go with the program when she rode with him.

As they drove home through the quiet countryside Jodi said sleepily, "Thanks for letting me go with you, Dad. That was fun."

His eyes never leaving the road, her father reached over to ruffle her straight, blond hair. "No problem. You're good company when you're not being a pain." He grinned widely as she gasped in mock indignation.

Jodi was half asleep by the time they pulled into the driveway.

Deputy Sheriff Dan Itri in the field behind his house.

Household Maneuvers

"Pizza-Hut-can-I-help-you?" said the rushed voice on the phone. The Pizza Hut on Main Street in Fredericksburg was always busy. It was the only one for miles.

Jodi asked, "Can I speak to Eileen please?"

"Hold on." Jodi tapped her foot impatiently as a Pizza Hut ad played into her ear. Finally her mother picked up. "This is Eileen."

"Hi Mom, it's me. Can I go spend the night at Skyla's? She already asked her mom and it's okay." There was a short pause as her mother considered it. Jodi could hear pans clanging and things beeping in the background, and she pictured her mom standing in her Pizza Hut uniform, short and sweating, hair skinned back in a limp ponytail. "Please?" she pleaded.

"I guess so . . ." her mother said, raising Jodi's hopes before adding, "but you'll have to check with Dad first."

"Oh, Mom! You know he never likes me to go anywhere. He'll just say no."

"I've got to go, Jodi. I'm in the middle of rolling out a crust."

Jodi sighed as she hung up the phone. Her dad was in his workshop. He earned extra money on his days off by repairing other people's cars—he could fix almost anything—but he didn't like being interrupted when he was working.

This would take some planning.

Jodi considered for a moment, then went into the

kitchen to pour a tall glass of iced tea. It was a warm day, and he was probably thirsty. Maybe it would put him in a good mood. She carried it carefully out the front door and across the grassy field to his workshop, glancing at her Pawpaw's small red and white helicopter as she passed. That was another thing her dad was working on, trying to get it ready to sell. He and Pawpaw had built it from a kit several years before.

"Dad?" she called out, stepping carefully into the two-car garage workshop. "I brought you some tea!"

Her father slid out from under a car and sat up, wiping his greasy hands on a rag. "Thanks. Is there some reason I'm getting this special treatment?" The quizzical look he gave her wasn't encouraging. He was already suspicious.

"Uh, no reason. So what are you doing with the car?"

"Overhauling the engine."

"Really? How do you do that?"

"Well, you have to pull the engine out, drain the oil and water and drop the oil pan, then pull the rod and main caps off and look at the bearings to see how bad they are. Then you have to see if the crankshaft needs turning."

Jodi listened attentively, her eyes almost crossing from boredom. "Wow. So is there anything else I can get you?"

Mr. Itri fixed Jodi with the same piercing look he used when he was in uniform. "You want to stop pretending to be interested in cars and tell me what you really want?"

"Oh. Well, Skyla called and invited me to spend the night. Mom already said it was okay with her if it was okay with you."

"What are you going to do there?"

The question caught her off-guard. "Watch movies, I guess. And I think it might be her father's birthday. Anyway, she said her mom could pick me up, so you wouldn't even have to drive me there!"

Her father sounded irritated. "I'm working this weekend. I want you to stay home so your mom won't be here by herself."

"But Dad, I—"

"The answer's no. You've been away the last two weekends."

"But Lisa gets to be gone all the time—"

"Lisa's five years older than you. I said no, and that's final."

Jodi matched his look with a piercing look of her own. "Okay, fine. Whatever. I guess I'll be in my room like always!" Stiff with fury, she stalked back toward the house.

A loud, squalling cry of "Ma-aa" suddenly came from the pen beside the house. Jodi turned aside with an exasperated sigh. Her goat, Payback, wanted her attention.

She leaned over the chain-link gate to scratch his head. "What's your problem? I already fed you today." Payback gave her a pitiful look, and Jodi smiled in spite of herself. "You're a spoiled brat, you know that?"

The goat had been an Easter present from her aunt, who claimed it was a pay back for all the puppies and kittens Jodi's mom had given her kids at Easter. Jodi had promptly named the bouncy young kid Payback. Her Easter goat had tried to follow her into the house one time, and another time he tried to get into the car with her! He was clueless.

"Maybe you'll get lucky today and Mom will bring home some leftover pizza for you," Jodi told him. Payback happily butted her hand.

By the time her mom came home that afternoon, Jodi was resigned to staying home for the weekend. Once her dad made up his mind about something, that was it. He was tough.

She perched on a bar stool at the kitchen counter to watch her mother work. She was a fantastic cook. "What are you making?"

"Jalapeno casserole."

"Yum! I'm starving." Jodi picked up a paper napkin and started shredding it. "Dad said I couldn't go to Skyla's."

Her mother glanced up. "I figured, since you were still here. Don't be too upset. You know he works long hours. I think he misses spending time with you."

Jodi didn't answer. She liked doing things with her dad, even though it was usually helping him around the house. She once spent weeks holding boards for him while he cut them with a jigsaw, then she held wood panels against the wall while he nailed them. They'd painted and paneled the whole back room by themselves. It turned out great.

By the time her father came in for dinner, Jodi was in a better mood. "Did you get the car done?" she asked politely. She could tell he was tired.

"I think so. I'm done with it for the day, anyway." He ate a few bites and said to his wife, "Mama, I'm going to go hover the helicopter after dinner for a bit, and I need you to videotape it for me."

"All right," she replied. Jodi hid a smile. Her dad always insisted that his "maneuvers" with the helicopter be videotaped so he could check to see how it was handling. They ended up with thirty-minute videos of him doing the exact same things over and over: going up about eighteen inches, moving forward, moving backward, and maybe turning in place from time to time. Until he got his pilot's license, he couldn't take it up any farther.

Her dad's eyes slid to her. "Jodi, you want to ride in the helicopter with me?"

She quickly shook her head. "No way! That thing scares me."

Dan Itri in the copter.   The experimental craft.

"Oh, come on. It's fun! You're not turning into a wuss, are you?"

"Whatever, so I'm a wuss. I'm not getting in that thing."

He tried a few more times to persuade her, but she was firm. That was one thing about her dad; anytime he got excited about something, he wanted to share it with her. He loved playing with the helicopter, so he was sure she would too.

A few minutes later Jodi heard the sputtering sound of the motor starting up. She glanced out the front door and saw her dad in the seat of the little helicopter, rotors already slicing through the air. From the doorway, she could just make out the black letters across the side: "EXPERIMENTAL." Her mom stood nearby with her eye to the video camera.

Jodi closed the door and decided to watch TV instead. How exciting could another practice flight be?

Silent Crash

The television in the living room drowned out the noise of the crash.

It was several weeks later. Jodi was sprawled comfortably on the couch watching TV when the front door burst open and her father ran inside.

"Jodi, get your shoes on real quick!" he snapped. "I need your help!"

She was already moving. "What's going on?"

"Car wreck," he said tersely. "Out on the highway. It

looks like somebody's down on the road. Hurry up!"

Their long dirt driveway ran along some trees and past a barbed wire fence to the highway. A moment later, Jodi was pounding along the driveway behind her dad. He had been out in his workshop when he heard the crash. They were close enough to see a crumpled black Ford Explorer.

Jodi's heart was racing. She had listened to her dad talk about accidents and first aid almost all her life, but she'd never actually seen a badly injured person. She wasn't sure she could handle it.

But she was a cop's daughter, and her father was counting on her. She determined to follow his lead and do what needed to be done.

When they reached the highway, Jodi saw a woman lying on the pavement, her arms out to her sides. She had blood on her face and arms, but her eyes were open. It looked like she'd been thrown out of the Explorer.

Jodi knelt beside her and took her hand. "Are you okay?" she asked.

The woman's black hair was fanned out on the pavement. She mumbled something but didn't move. Jodi looked around for her dad, afraid she might do the wrong thing. She knew you shouldn't try to move an injured person. She held the woman's hand and tried to reassure her until the ambulance arrived.

After the ambulance left and they started back up the driveway to the house, Jodi was unusually quiet. Her father looked down at her quizzically. "Hey Brat, are you okay?"

"I guess so. That was scary."

He smiled down at her. "Well, you did a good job."

"Really?" Jodi's spirits lifted. "All I did was tell her to stay still. She acted real confused."

"I'm sure she was. You wouldn't believe some of the crazy things people do after car wrecks. Sometimes they walk or crawl right out into traffic! People in shock don't know what they're doing."

"Why? Because they get hit in the head?"

"No, it's different from a head injury. Shock happens when you don't have enough blood flowing through your whole body, like if you're bleeding a lot or badly dehydrated. It can shut you down fast. We always have to watch for that in accidents."

"What do you do about it?"

Mr. Itri shrugged. "Depends on what's causing it. We call for an ambulance and try to stop the bleeding or whatever if we can see it. And if the person's completely out of it, running around in traffic, we try to keep them from killing themselves." He grinned. "I've had to chase people down more than once."

His words made her feel better. She hadn't done CPR or anything, but maybe she'd helped the woman more than she thought by staying calm and keeping her still.

Caught on Tape

A delicious smell filled the air. "Where's Ali?" asked Mrs. Itri as Jodi wandered into the kitchen to see what was cooking.

"She's back in my room." Ali, Jodi's younger cousin, had flown in from California the week before for a visit. She and Jodi spent much of their time exploring the nearby fields and woods. "I think I wore her out."

The front door slammed, and Don Itri walked in. "Mama? Can I get you to come outside for a few minutes? I'm going to hover the helicopter, and I need you to video-tape it."

Mrs. Itri sighed and turned off the stove. "I'll be right there."

Jodi went back to her room. A few minutes later, she and Ali heard the helicopter start. They ignored it and continued to chat.

Outside, Eileen Itri stood patiently with the video camera to her eye, following the movements of the small helicopter as it skimmed back and forth across the grass. Her husband sat at the controls wearing a dark baseball cap and long-sleeved white shirt. Through the camera's small lens she could see him smiling under his bushy mustache. He really liked these "test flights."

After twenty minutes, though, she'd had enough. A few times she let the camera drift away from the helicopter to show the surrounding field, the workshop and even Payback. She sighed. She really should get back to cook-ing supper.

She pointed the camera back at the helicopter. It made another low hop, then settled down in the grass at a slight angle. The left skid touched the ground, then seemed to shudder. It had settled into a dip in the field. Her husband leaned out a few inches to look down at the skid.

Just then, something dark flew across in front of the camera.

Mrs. Itri frowned. What was that, a buzzard? She moved the camera away from her eye and squinted toward the helicopter. It looked like her husband was still staring down at the skid. The helicopter was definitely tilted to the left now, the rotor slicing through the air at an angle. She mentally shrugged and put the camera back to her eye. He'd holler if he wanted her to stop taping.

After another few moments she took the camera away again. Why wasn't he moving? It almost looked like he was—

That's when she saw the blood.

With a gasp, she dropped the camera on the grass and ran toward the helicopter. Her husband was sagging sideways through the open doorway, blood gushing down his face and onto his white shirt, his head only inches from the whirling blades. The only thing holding him in was the seat belt. His cap was crumpled nearby on the grass—the "buzzard" that had shot past her lens. A piece of the tail rotor, a jagged metal blade over a foot long, was also lying on the grass, its edges stained with blood.

"Dad!" she screamed. "Dad! Oh no . . ." With the rotors almost hitting the ground beside him, there was no way she could fit under them to help him. After a frozen moment she ran for the house.

"Jodi!" she shouted. "Jodi, call nine-one-one! Your dad's hurt real bad! And bring out a towel!"

Inside, Jodi looked at Ali in astonishment and then grabbed the phone. She stabbed the three numbers and quickly told the dispatcher to send an ambulance. They all knew where the Itris lived.

She slammed down the phone, grabbed a towel and hit the front door running.

Steel Blades

Eileen Itri was on her hands and knees, trying desperately to find a way under the blades. Jodi's stomach lurched when she saw how close her mother was to the whirring steel. There wasn't room for an adult to squeeze past.

The whole side of the helicopter was glistening with blood. It only took a glance to see that her father was badly hurt. As she stared, he suddenly shifted in the seat and groaned, then started fumbling with the seat belt. If he tried to get out he'd fall right into the blades.

She sprinted for the helicopter shouting, "Dad, turn it off! Turn it off, Dad!" She reached her mother's side and roughly pulled her away, then flung herself flat on the ground. She was small enough to fit under the rotor—just barely—as long as she hugged the ground.

"Turn it off!" she continued to plead as she wormed her way toward him. The wind from the blades beat down on her, flattening the grass and filling her ears with a popping sound. She didn't dare lift her head.

As she reached the open door of the helicopter and

looked up, her father groaned again and shifted in his seat, toppling even farther out. "No!" she shrieked in a panic, rising to her knees to block his way out. "Stop! Turn it off! Please, Dad!"

He acted like he didn't hear her. He fumbled again for the seat belt, and this time his fingers found the metal clasp. The belt parted and fell open on his lap.

Now the only thing that stood between him and the blades was Jodi.

She threw all her weight against her father's much larger frame, trying to shove him back inside. He mumbled something and turned toward her, and for the first time she saw his face. His left cheek was hanging open like a piece of meat, his eye filled with blood. His jaw was hanging open, blood spilling from his lips. It looked like his face had been cut in half.

Jodi gasped and looked away in horror. A wave of nausea hit her, leaving her lightheaded. This can't be happening, she thought, fighting to stay calm. She felt small and helpless. She couldn't even hear her mother's shouts any more over the throbbing sound of the rotor. It was just her and her dad.

It was up to her.

The thought brought resolve. Somehow she had to stop the helicopter before her dad got past her to the blades, and she also had to keep him from bleeding to death until the ambulance got there. She was still holding the towel in one hand, so she used it to press her father's cheek back in place. She pressed hard, both to keep him inside the helicopter and to stop the bleeding. She could hardly bear to look at him. The metallic smell of blood was making her sick.

Instead, she looked around the small cockpit. Keys dangled from a switch inside, but the control stick was right in front of her in the doorway. She was terrified that if she bumped it, the helicopter would take off. To get to the keys she would have to lean directly across the stick.

She was debating what to do when her father mumbled something and lurched against her, knocking her back toward the blades. Jodi shrieked and pushed him back.

"Please don't move!" she sobbed, somehow managing to keep the towel against his face. "I'm trying to help you, Dad."

The towel was already soaked through with blood. She realized he must be in shock. She didn't know if he could even hear her. "Dad, stay in there!" she pleaded. "Stop trying to come out! You're gonna get cut!"

Her mother's frantic voice pierced through the rotor noise. "Don, we need you to turn it off!" she shouted. *"Turn it off!"*

Jodi knew she couldn't hold him in much longer. She had to stop the blades. Planting her right arm and shoulder against her father's chest, she leaned across him and reached for the keys with her left hand. The instant her fingers closed around them she twisted them toward her to the "off" position.

Nothing happened.

"How do I turn it off, Dad?" she asked desperately.

"Help me turn it off!" Eyes darting, she finally noticed a black toggle switch next to the keys. It was flipped up. Without thinking, she leaned in and slapped it down.

The helicopter's engine abruptly sputtered and died.

Relief flooded through her. The rotor would stop, and she could get her dad out to safety. The ambulance should be there any second.

But her relief was short-lived. Even with the engine off, the blades continued to slice through the air in a deadly blur. It would take time for them to slow down and stop.

She didn't know how much more time she had. Her father's struggle to escape was turning frantic. He mumbled louder and louder and tried repeatedly to shove his way past her. He didn't know where he was, and he had only one idea in his semiconscious state—to get out.

"Stay in there, Dad!" Jodi begged tearfully. "Stay! The propellers are going to hit you!"

In an advanced state of shock, Don Itri was too agitated to understand what she was saying, or even who she was. He had a policeman's build and strength, and even in his weakened condition, he was more than a match for a scrawny thirteen year old. With a hoarse shout, he forced his way past Jodi and tumbled out of the helicopter.

Time slowed to a crawl as Jodi stumbled backward shrieking, "No, Dad. No!" She braced herself for the bite of the razor sharp blades. They were still moving fast enough to cut off her head. She instinctively collapsed into a crouch, head down, and pulled her father down with her. It took her a moment to realize they were both still alive, huddled inches below the blades.

"Get down!" she screamed in her father's ear as he fought to stand. "The propellers will cut you all up! Stay down, don't move!" She shoved the towel back against his face, which was once again pouring blood.

Whether he suddenly recognized her voice or was just too weak from loss of blood and the effort he'd just made, he quit struggling. Jodi huddled there with him until the blades slowed almost to a stop, then helped him crawl out and away from the helicopter.

Eileen Itri was sobbing hysterically. Jodi kept the towel pressed hard to her father's face, only vaguely aware of others milling around—a neighbor, her cousin, and eventually paramedics and a crowd of her father's friends from the police force.

It wasn't until her father was loaded into the ambulance and the doors slammed shut that her hands began to shake. Standing outside in the hot Texas sun, she wrapped herself in her own arms as if against a chill.

Six Months Later

"Hey Brat, how about bringing me a glass of ice tea?"

Jodi smiled. For some reason, her father was stubbornly determined to rebuild the small helicopter and fly it again. He'd been working on it for days.

"Okay!" she called as she strolled toward the house.

After hundreds of stitches and months of recovery, Don Itri was happy to finally be back at work with the Sheriff's

Department. The surgery, performed by a cosmetic surgeon called in by the hospital, had left amazingly few scars on his face.

Jodi brought him his tea, then hung around to watch. She didn't have to pretend to be interested in the helicopter—since the crash, she had replayed the scene a million times in her head. She pointed to the control stick next to the door. "Dad, what would've happened if I'd moved that?"

Mr. Itri raised an eyebrow. "Most likely it would've made the copter jump and cut both our heads off," he said calmly. "It's a good thing you didn't do that."

Well. That was one thing she could say about her dad; he didn't tone things down for her like she was a baby. He was strong, and he expected her to be strong. A cop's daughter.

"You feel like riding with me tonight?" Mr. Itri asked.

"Sure!" she answered quickly. She hadn't ridden with him since he'd gone back to work.

That night they rode in companionable silence up and down the country roads and downtown streets. It was almost midnight when they pulled into Jek's Pit Stop, an all-night convenience store in Fredericksburg and a favorite stop for cops on the late-night shift. Several other officers were already inside drinking coffee and eating donuts.

"I'll just wander around inside while you drink your coffee, okay?" Jodi said as they walked in. Sometimes her dad wanted to talk to his friends without having a teenager hanging around.

"No, I want you to stay with me," he replied sternly. Jodi looked up in surprise as he deliberately turned her to face his friends across the room. Her face turned red as they looked up and stared at her, but her father just smiled.

"This," he announced loudly enough so the whole store could hear, "is the daughter who saved my life!"

That was all the thanks Jodi would ever need.

Jodi and her parents at the awards ceremony.

Jodi Itri received the Department of Transportation's National Heroism Award for "placing her life at risk to save another person." She hung the plaque in the hallway outside her bedroom door.

Would You Know What to Do . . . for Someone in Shock?

Take this quiz and find out!

1. **Your body goes into a life-threatening state of shock when:**
   a. you receive a hard blow to the head
   b. your heart and blood vessels can't pump enough oxygen-rich blood to all parts of your body
   c. you're hurt and unconscious
   d. you learn your mom won *Survivor* and your friends now think she's cooler than you

2. **Some common symptoms of shock include:**
   a. bags under your eyes
   b. paleness, confusion, restlessness and irritability
   c. muscle spasms in face
   d. b and c

3. **Blood-volume related (hypovolemic) shock can be caused by:**
   a. heavy bleeding from an internal or external wound
   b. diarrhea
   c. severe vomiting
   d. all the above

4. **Heart-related (cardiogenic) shock can be caused by:**
   a. exercising too hard
   b. any disease or event that keeps the heart from pumping enough blood to all parts of the body
   c. taking aspirin in the early stages of a heart attack
   d. getting dumped on Valentine's Day

5. **Toxin-related (septic) shock can be caused by:**
   a. eating moldy cheese
   b. biting your nails
   c. a severe bacterial infection
   d. the cafeteria's mystery meat

6. **Allergy-related (anaphylactic) shock can be caused by:**
   a. not washing your hands before you eat
   b. a compound fracture of your femur
   c. a bee sting
   d. a and c

7. **The first goal in the treatment of shock is to:**
   a. recognize that the person is in shock
   b. clear the person's airway by tilting his/her head back
   c. place a pillow or folded cloth under the head to make him/her feel more relaxed
   d. call the newspaper, since you're planning to be a hero

8. **Once you recognize that a person is in shock, you should immediately:**
   a. begin CPR or rescue breathing
   b. call 911 or have someone else call 911
   c. put a cool, damp cloth on his/her forehead
   d. check the color of his/her fingernails to see if they're blue

9. **The second goal in the treatment of shock is to:**
   a. call, or have someone else call, the person's relatives
   b. slap the person to make them "snap out of it"
   c. identify and stop the underlying condition if possible (i.e. stop severe bleeding, remove source of heat if it's a burn, etc.)
   d. make sure the person doesn't move his/her neck

10. **Once the underlying condition is stopped, it can help slow the progression of shock to:**
    a. raise the person's legs to improve blood flow to the brain
    b. keep the person from getting chilled or overheated
    c. loosen tight clothing around the neck, chest and waist
    d. all the above

11. **If a person in shock asks for a drink of water, you should:**
    a. give them as much as they want; they might be dehydrated
    b. give them a little, but in small sips
    c. don't give them anything to drink, but moisten their lips to make them more comfortable
    d. ask if they'd prefer Evian or Perrier

12. **If the state of shock is left untreated, the person will:**
    a. die
    b. suffer brain damage
    c. eventually recover on their own
    d. recover much more quickly without your interference

13. **A similar, but less serious (temporary, not usually life-threatening) stress-related (psychogenic) "shock-like condition" can be caused by:**
    a. learning that you've won the Publisher's Clearing-house Sweepstakes
    b. walking through the perfume section of the department store
    c. watching a dog get hit by a car
    d. a and c

14. **If a person in shock is irritable and aggressive to the point of attempting to hit those trying to help, you should:**
    a. enlist help from others and try to wrestle him/her to the ground
    b. send the biggest, strongest helper to get the person under control
    c. stay back and protect yourself
    d. place bets on how long it'll take before he/she collapses

15. **If a noisy crowd gathers around the shocked person and upsets him/her, you should:**
    a. ask if there's a medically trained person in the crowd
    b. ask others to please step back and be quiet
    c. use a calm voice to reassure the person in shock
    d. all the above

Answers: 1-b, 2-b, 3-d, 4-b, 5-c, 6-c, 7-a, 8-b, 9-c, 10-d, 11-c, 12-a, 13-d, 14-c, 15-d

Give yourself five points for each correct answer, then check your score below:

70–75: *Teens 911 Top Gun.* You've demonstrated an unusually high level of knowledge and skills. Congratulations!

60–65: You've demonstrated an above-average level of knowledge and skills. Not bad.

50–55: While you've demonstrated at least some basic knowledge, it's not enough to keep you (or someone you're trying to help) out of trouble.

45 or Below: If you come across someone in shock, do them a big favor and just call 911! They'll have enough problems without being slapped or tackled.

River of No Return

When help is nowhere to be found on a rafting trip gone awry, two brothers join forces to bring their father home.

andy Hall, sixteen, ran his fingers lightly over the top of his head, feeling the spiky tips of his newly cut hair with satisfaction. He'd gone to Rage, a popular salon in Burley, Idaho, and asked for a new look. He really liked what they'd done.

Back at home, he admired his hair one more time in his bedroom mirror before grabbing the car keys and heading out. He barely glanced at his fourteen-year-old brother, Curtis, as they passed in the hallway, but what he saw was enough to bring him to a screeching halt.

Curtis was sporting an identical new haircut.

"You cut your hair just like mine!" Randy yelled angrily. "I can't believe this! Who said you could have a haircut like me?"

Curtis set his jaw. "I can get my hair cut any way I want! Since when do I need *your* permission?"

Randy's face was flushed. "It's bad enough that you dress like me half the time, but no way am I going to have matching haircuts with my little brother!" People were always getting them mixed up because they were both very tall with similar features. The last thing they needed was matching hair!

He stepped forward, deliberately crowding Curtis. If there was one thing they did well, it was fight. It usually ended up with one of them face down on the carpet in a headlock while their mom tried to pull them apart.

Randy thought it was time for Curtis to eat carpet fuzz.

"Hey look, I didn't know!" Curtis said quickly, correctly interpreting his brother's intention. He didn't have time for a typical Hall versus Hall encounter. He had stuff to do.

"Yeah, right," Randy snapped. "Just stay out of my way."

He stormed into the bathroom and started furiously combing his hair to make it look different.

Curtis shrugged and went downstairs, lured by the smell of fresh-baked chocolate chip cookies. Pam Hall, a teacher at Dworshak Elementary School, spent most Saturdays baking and house-cleaning. She'd always made it a point to keep the tall owl-shaped

Randy Hall showing off his bike.

cookie jar on the counter filled with fresh cookies, a tradition all five of her kids had enjoyed.

"Mmmm," Curtis murmured cheerfully as he slipped in beside her to steal a spoonful of cookie dough. "Way to go, Mom!"

Mrs. Hall smiled up at him. All her sons were tall, the older ones topping six-foot-six. "So what was all the yelling upstairs about?" she asked.

"Randy and I both got our hair cut today, and we ended up with the same style. He thinks I did it on purpose, like I'd *want* to look like him!"

"Be nice," she said automatically. "You two are going to have to work it out, so don't make it harder than it has to be."

"Uh-huh." Curtis clinked his licked-clean spoon in the sink. "I think I'm going to go play basketball."

"Are you going to clean your room?"

Curtis grinned. "Sure! Sometime. Just not now." He left quickly before she could get tough. She wasn't a natural disciplinarian like his dad. She had to really work at it. She'd rather bake cookies and crochet little baby hats than scold kids. A perfect mother.

His father, Ron Hall, was a manager at the Albertson's in Burley. He worked long hours six days a week and was usually exhausted by the time he got home. On his few days off, he spent most of his time building model trains and assembling intricate tracks and scenery in his "train room." He wasn't much into the outdoors.

I'll bet Dad's dreading the rafting trip coming up, Curtis thought as he tossed the basketball from hand to hand. He

Curtis shooting hoops.

and Randy were both Boy Scouts, and their troop would be whitewater rafting down the Salmon River the end of July. Since the boys couldn't go unless their dads went, Mr. Hall had reluctantly agreed to go on the five-day trip.

Curtis loved camping, hiking and mountain biking with his troop. He just hoped Randy would stay out of his face—and out of his raft!

Into the Wilderness

"Do you have everything?" Mrs. Hall asked nervously as Randy, Curtis and Mr. Hall shoved their sleeping bags and other supplies into a van bursting with teenage boys.

Each family was supposed to bring one camping meal big enough to serve the whole group on the trip down-river, so Mrs. Hall had prepared a take-along breakfast: bacon, hash browns, bread and a milk jug filled with a French toast mix of raw scrambled eggs. She'd frozen it all and packed it into a chest with dry ice so it would last a few days.

Ron Hall checked off the items. "I guess we're ready to go." He glanced at the van, still less than thrilled at the thought of five days in the wilderness.

"Have a good trip!" Mrs. Hall quickly kissed her husband and sons good-bye, but as she stepped back, she felt a sudden stab of anxiety. "Be careful!"

She waved as the van rolled out of sight, then slowly turned back toward the house. Her sudden nervousness troubled her. Her sons were in good hands,

Randy and his mom.

especially with their father along. She told herself there was nothing to worry about.

Inside the van, Curtis and Randy were ignoring each other, getting in practice for the rest of the trip. Their first stop would be eighty miles down the road in Pocatello, where they would pick up the rafts they'd reserved. The rented rafts were inflatable sixteen-footers made to comfortably hold six adults.

"Do we get to pick who we raft with?" Randy asked Mr. Tufts, the driver of the van.

"I think the plan is for fathers and sons to team up," he replied. "You and Curtis will ride with your dad, and you'll probably have a couple of others with you. We have to fit everybody into five rafts."

"Great," Randy muttered. "I get stuck with my little brother."

"Knock it off," Mr. Hall said.

Randy settled back. It was going to be an all-day ride to Corn Creek, where the road literally ended in the middle of Idaho's No Return Wilderness and the roller-coaster rapids of the Salmon River began. They'd camp overnight on the riverbank and launch the rafts the next morning.

It was after nine o'clock that night when the vans rolled into the clearing at Corn Creek. The campers wearily unloaded the rafts and boating supplies onto the dock, then dragged their tents and sleeping bags to a flat area blanketed with pine needles.

Randy and Curtis picked spots for the two dome tents. "I'm staying in my own tent," Randy declared, kicking some sticks out of the way.

"Sure," Mr. Hall replied. "Curtis can sleep in the tent with me."

"Wait a minute, why should he get his own tent?" Curtis protested. "He always gets stuff just because he's older!"

"That's right," Mr. Hall said unsympathetically.

Curtis glared at Randy. It wasn't fair that Randy always got the best deal—he got to go more places and stay out later, and he always had more money. Just for once he'd like to come out ahead on something.

"Hey Curt, can you grab the other side of my tent and pull?" Randy's small dome tent had doubled over on itself.

Curtis gave him a scornful look. "Why don't you do it yourself? It's your tent!" He deliberately turned his back.

By the time all the tents were pitched, everyone was exhausted. Soon the only sounds in the clearing were the rush of water and the rustling of the pine branches overhead.

@   @   @

Back at home in Burley, Pam Hall was tossing in her sleep. Suddenly she gasped and sat bolt upright, heart pounding wildly.

Something was wrong.

The boys. One of her sons was in horrible danger. She could *feel* it. Something bad was going to happen on this trip.

"No," she whispered aloud. "Please, Heavenly Father, I can't lose one of my sons. Protect them."

It took her hours to get back to sleep.

River of No Return

"Come on, boys, the sooner we get everything packed away the sooner we can leave! If you don't need something, go lock it in the cars."

The first rays of sunlight slanted through the trees and birds called overhead as Scoutmaster Alan Hunter tried to get the sleepy group moving. Randy already had his tent packed away and strapped to the raft. Curtis was carrying his duffel out onto the dock when he spotted a huge, dark shape swimming across the river just upstream.

"Hey, look, a moose!" he exclaimed. Everyone ran over and watched the enormous animal climb out on the far bank. It ignored them and moved into the forest, dripping wet.

"Cool," Curtis said admiringly. It was a perfect way to start the trip.

Once everything was strapped under the stretchy nets in the rafts, the whole group walked over to the ranger's station for a safety briefing. They listened impatiently, anxious to get underway.

"Mother Nature can be very unforgiving when you're out in the wilderness," the ranger warned them. "Lewis and Clark nicknamed the Salmon the 'River of No Return' because once you get a few miles downstream, there's no turning back. The wild rapids and rugged terrain go on for hundreds of miles. It's some of the roughest wilderness in all of North America.

"When Lewis and Clark explored this area, they had to pull over at almost every bend to look at the rapids ahead so they'd know what they were getting into. You'll have maps to show you what to expect, but you'll still have to be careful. If you get snagged in a logjam, your chances of getting out unscathed are pretty slim.

"Watch out for changes in the river level, and leave the wildlife alone. You're going into their country, so you have to play by their rules. You're likely to see everything from rattlesnakes to bears to moose, so store your food up high in bear sacks and keep your campsites clean.

"And while we're talking about keeping things clean, always go above the highest waterline before you go to the bathroom or even brush your teeth. Every living creature along the Salmon is dependent on the water to survive.

"Keep your life jackets on while you're on the river. Stay alert, watch out for each other, and have fun!"

With a cheer, the boys rushed for the rafts, and after a few minutes of laughter and splashing, they were ready to go. Mr. Hunter would ride in front to watch for "sleepers" —hidden rocks—and pick the best rapids. Randy, Curtis and Mr. Hall were sharing their raft with fourteen-year-old John Anderson and his father, Ray. The Hansens would ride in the last raft, which carried a boat repair kit and first aid kit.

Curtis and Randy settled into their blue rubber raft, jostling for the best seats. One by one, the five groups pushed off and caught the current, using paddles to steer clear of rocks.

"You doing okay, Dad?" Randy asked as they bobbed along behind the first three rafts. It would be hours before they would reach the first real rapids, but after that it would get exciting. The Salmon River cascaded down through the Sawtooth Mountains at a breakneck pace, cutting through a gorge deeper than the Grand Canyon. The Scoutmaster had a map that showed all the landmarks and rapids.

"Sure," Mr. Hall replied. Randy could tell he was nervous about the whole thing, but he was being a good sport.

Curtis was busy taking in the scenery. The riverbanks varied in color as they went along, light gray in some areas and nearly black in others. The woods on both sides were thick and tangled, their shadowy depths easily able to hide bears or cougars. He could almost feel the gaze of unseen eyes as they floated past in the warm sunshine.

Two hours and twelve miles later, the sun was high in the sky and everyone was starving. They pulled to shore along a level stretch of riverbank wide enough so they could all sit down. The family who'd brought lunch for the day opened coolers and passed out sandwich makings, only to discover that they'd left all the lunch meat behind. A chorus of groans went up from the hungry teens.

"What are we supposed to eat, mustard sandwiches?" Randy joked, waving an empty hoagie roll. The groans quickly turned to good-natured laughter, though, as the boys devoured the rolls, corn chips and cupcakes down to the last crumb.

They were still talking and laughing when a distant buzz caught their attention. Like a mosquito zooming in on a picnic, it seemed to be getting closer. Soon a sleek jet boat appeared and roared past them, the driver waving a friendly greeting. Within seconds it was out of sight.

The Scoutmaster had been studying his map. "Okay, listen up everybody! Devil's Teeth Rapid will be coming up in about an hour. It'll be our first three-point-five rapid." Rapids were rated according to the water levels and difficulty. "We need to clean up here and get every-thing strapped back down. Let's go!"

A few gray clouds were skidding across the sky as they pushed off down the river, but if anyone noticed the clouds it was with thankfulness for the brief shade they gave from the hot summer sun.

Into the Devil's Teeth

"Yeah!" Curtis yelled, gripping his paddle with both hands as the raft bounced and porpoised through the rapids. He and John Anderson were at the front, with Randy and the two dads at the back. They were all using their paddles to steer through the twists and turns.

Randy grinned and used the flat of his paddle to splash Curtis from behind, catching him by surprise, but when Curtis tried to retaliate, the dads made him stop since he was also splashing them. Randy grinned even wider. He was immune!

"I'm gonna swim for a while," Randy said. "It's getting hot." He put down his paddle and rolled over the side into the rushing water, and soon boys from the other rafts joined him. They had no trouble keeping up; the biggest problem was not getting too far ahead. The current swept them along at a brisk pace.

Once he was cooled off, Randy grabbed the side of his raft and hauled himself back in, splashing his dad and Mr. Anderson in the process. In the hot sun, though, it didn't take long to dry out.

Up front, Curtis and John also took turns tumbling out of the raft and floating along beside it. By the time they'd all been in and out a few times, they were getting tired. Randy finally had to ask his dad for help; he was too exhausted to pull himself into the raft.

Mr. Hall looked down at him and laughed. "You've already splashed us half a dozen times getting in and out. You wanted in, you can stay in!"

"C'mon Dad!" Randy protested. His father pretended to study the sky. "Oh, man," Randy grumbled. With rubbery arms he just managed to slide back into the raft. He decided he was done swimming for a while. He leaned back, enjoying the warmth of the midafternoon sun.

Suddenly it seemed like the very air around them darkened. Randy glanced up to see huge black clouds rolling in overhead. They cast the whole river into shadow.

"Looks like a storm's coming up," Curtis said. With each passing second the sky turned blacker and the wind picked up. Curtis shielded his face with his hand, watching the rafts ahead. The water and trees suddenly looked strange, almost like night had fallen in the middle of the afternoon. He felt uneasy. There was something menacing, almost personal, about this storm. He tugged on his life jacket straps to make sure they were tight.

Over the next few minutes, the wind rose to hurricane force, literally howling up the canyon and whipping the already frothing water into waves. It was all Curtis could do to hang on. If he let go, he would be blown over backwards. He'd never seen anything like it.

Randy and Mr. Hall yelled something from the back of the raft, but the roaring wind tore away their voices.

"What?" Curtis yelled. A wave splashed over the front of the raft, slamming into him before pooling at his feet. Eyes stinging from wind and water, he peered ahead at the other rafts.

At first he couldn't believe his eyes. The wind was literally blowing them back upstream, against the current!

It was impossible, but it was happening. He glanced back at Randy, and this time he didn't need to hear his words to get the idea. They needed to get to the shore.

Even with all five of them paddling as hard as they could, it was a struggle to turn the raft aside. They headed for the only clearing they could see, a small rocky area at the foot of a steep embankment. As soon as the front of the raft scraped bottom, Curtis jumped out and grabbed the lead rope, but it was like trying to hold a bucking bronco. The wind and current fought over the raft like a toy, making it fishtail wildly. Curtis found himself being dragged back into the water.

"Randy!" he yelled in a panic, but his brother was already on the way. He jumped onto the shore and closed his hands over the rope behind Curtis's hands. Together, they were able to hold the raft.

"Is there anywhere to tie it off?" Randy shouted. "If we pull it up on these rocks we might put a hole in the side!"

Curtis nodded toward a boulder nearby. "Over there!" Even standing with their shoulders touching, the wind was so loud they could barely hear each other. Curtis's arms were straining against the rope until it felt like they were being pulled out of their sockets. "I'll try to give you some slack so you can tie it! You ready?"

"Do it!"

It was blowing impossibly hard, rippling the dark tree-tops like giant waves and filling the air with dust and water spray. Onboard the raft, Ron Hall and Ray and John Anderson were hastily shoving the paddles and bottles of sunscreen under the net before the wind could snatch them away. Once everything was secure, Mr. Hall climbed into the water and ducked behind the side of the raft, using it as a windbreak a few feet offshore.

Curtis leaned back against the rope, glancing to his left as Randy tried unsuccessfully to force a loop around the boulder. They were still struggling with it when Randy suddenly stared up in alarm at the embankment behind them. Curtis instinctively turned to follow his brother's gaze.

The next few seconds were a terrifying blur. Curtis peered up over his right shoulder to see a huge, dark boulder the size of a truck tire rolling and bouncing down the steep slope directly toward him and his brother. There was no time to run. He dropped the rope and threw himself aside, putting his hands up to cover his head.

On the last bounce before it reached them, literally inches above their heads, the boulder cracked in half with a sound like a pistol shot. One razor sharp piece hit Curtis's right forearm in a glancing blow, gashing it almost to the bone before flying on like a guided missile to the raft where the Andersons still sat. Mr. Anderson didn't even have time to duck. The heavy rock slammed into his leg like a cannonball, shattering the bone and knocking him backwards into the river before it tore through the raft and disappeared into the water.

The other half of the boulder was even more bent on destruction.

Curtis saw it as he lowered his hands, the first spattering of rain making him unaware that the wetness running down his right arm was blood. He watched in disbelief as the jagged chunk of rock bounced off the embankment and shot out across the water.

Straight as an arrow, but with far more deadly impact, it slammed into the side of his father's head.

Curtis's vision blurred with horror. When it cleared, he saw his father floating face down a few feet from shore, his body kept afloat only by the faded orange life jacket.

"Dad!" he shouted. Without hesitation, he plunged into the water. Randy was right behind him. Neither noticed the partially deflated raft or John Anderson straining to pull his injured father back onboard; all they could see was the apparently lifeless body of their own father.

The light rain was now blowing in a stinging barrage. The brothers plowed through the water to their father's side, and moving in unison, gripped his shoulders and flipped him over.

His eyes were wide open, his familiar features distorted and streaked with blood. Curtis froze, his eyes riveted to his father's face. A deep wound ran across the whole left side of his forehead and over his ear, and it looked like his nose was broken.

"Dad!" he gasped.

Mr. Hall blinked, then sucked in a huge gulp of air. He was alive!

"We've got you, Dad!" Randy shouted frantically over the wind's roar. "I love you!"

"I love you, Dad!" Curtis said. "Just hang on, all right?"

Blinking away the cold spray, the teens got a firm grip on him and fought their way back toward the rocky shore. "We need to get him up to a flat place!" Randy said. "Where's everybody else?"

Curtis looked around, but none of the other rafts was nearby. "Help!" he screamed. "Somebody get over here, we need help!" A wave of dizziness swept over him, and he suddenly staggered under his father's weight. He took another step with difficulty. What was wrong with him?

The wind-whipped water rinsed the blood from his arm and sent it swirling away in the rapids.

No Way Out

"Come on, Curt!" Randy snapped. He was straining, jaw clenched, to get his father onto the steep and rocky shore. He couldn't understand why Curtis was leaving all the lifting to him.

Curtis was lifting as hard as he could, but he felt strange. "I'm trying!" he said in frustration.

Finally Mr. Hansen, a dad from another raft, heard their shouts and splashed over to see what was wrong. One glance at Ron Hall was all it took. He stepped in and helped pull the injured man the rest of the way up onto the rocks.

Mr. Hall was still conscious, but just barely. He looked around in confusion. "I want to take my glasses off," he said, his hand fumbling toward his face. "My glasses . . ."

Randy caught his wrist and gently forced his hand down. "Don't touch your face, Dad. Your head is hurt. Just stay still." His father's sunglasses had come off in the river and were nowhere in sight.

"My glasses are . . . My glasses . . ." He was delirious. It looked like one part of his forehead was dented in. Randy looked at him helplessly, not sure what to do. He was afraid to even touch his head for fear of making it worse. Pressing on a skull fracture could push bone splinters into the brain.

"We need bandages," said Mr. Hansen. "Curtis, run back to my raft and get the first aid kit. It's about twenty yards upstream."

Curtis nodded, but when he turned to leave he couldn't decide the best route to take. If he tried to pick his way back upstream along the shore he'd be climbing wet boulders the whole way. Maybe it would be better if he climbed the embankment and worked his way back down. He hesitated, trying to focus. He felt like he was thinking through mud.

Randy watched him impatiently. "Never mind, I'll go! I'm faster than you anyway." Without hesitation, he headed for the boulders along the shoreline.

Curtis barely noticed. He decided to work his way over

along the embankment and . . . what was it he was supposed to get? He stared blankly at the rain-slick rocks tow-
ering above him. Oh yeah, the first aid kit. He started up
the slope, leaving a trail of bright red splotches on the
rocks behind him.

Mr. Hansen stared after Curtis, puzzled when the boy kept
climbing higher and higher. Several small rocks bounced
down after being dislodged by his feet. "Curtis!" he yelled.
"Come back down here! We don't need any rocks falling on
us!"

Curtis obeyed, turning automatically to retrace his
steps. It all seemed unreal—the rain, the river below, his
father sprawled like an injured soldier as Mr. Hansen bent
over him. Out on the river, Mr. Anderson was sitting on
the edge of their raft holding his leg, his face twisted in
pain. The rubber raft was partly deflated and wallowing in
the current. What had happened to it?

Farther downstream he saw several other people splashing their way toward the rocky clearing below. It was like
watching a movie from his vantage point above them.

"Curtis!" Mr. Hansen yelled again from below. Curtis
started moving again, placing his feet carefully on the
stones. By the time he made his way back down, Randy
was just returning.

"Here," Randy panted, setting down a five-gallon
bucket filled with first aid supplies. "The kit in your raft
was too small, so I got Mr. Hunter's."

"Good job. Let's bandage your dad's head and see if we
can stop the bleeding."

Several other Scouts and leaders arrived and scattered to find sticks to splint Mr. Anderson's broken leg. One man, Tom Miller, noticed the blood on Curtis's arm.

"It looks like you're bleeding," he said. "Let me see your arm."

Randy glanced up from awkwardly fitting a triangle bandage around his father's head. "That's probably Dad's blood. We were both holding on to him pretty tight."

Curtis nodded in agreement. "Don't worry about me. Just work on my dad."

Soon others were crowding onto the shore. In the confusion of wind and rain, none of them could figure out at first what had injured the two men. The rocks that had done all the damage were on the bottom of the river. They were astonished when Randy told them about the boulder, which had apparently split in half.

"The wind must've uprooted that tree at the top of the embankment, and that must've knocked a boulder loose," Alan Hunter speculated. "I've never seen a storm like this in my life. But how one boulder could hit two people who were that far apart and do this much damage . . . " He shook his head in disbelief.

Ron Hall was struggling to sit up. "Who are those people in the purple capes?" he asked fretfully. "Get them away from me! Get them away!" His unfocused eyes were gazing up the embankment.

"Purple capes? Uh, I don't know, Dad. Don't worry about them. Try to stay still." Randy placed another gauze square above his father's ear. As fast as he stuck them on, they turned scarlet with blood. He stacked on layer after layer and pressed gently, but nothing stopped the deadly flow. He was afraid to press any harder.

His father needed a hospital, doctors and blood. They had damp bandages in a five-gallon bucket. It seemed hopeless. Stranded in the middle of No Return Wilderness in rubber rafts, they were completely cut off from the outside world. Even if they managed to put together a makeshift stretcher, there was no way to raft back carrying him. The nearest help was miles upstream.

"We've got to do *something*," Mr. Hunter said. "Maybe we can send Tom downstream to find a phone. Let me grab my map . . . I know there's a ranch downstream, but I'm not sure how much farther it is."

After studying the map, though, he shook his head. "The closest stop is the Yellow Pine Ranch, but that's twenty-three miles downstream. It would take a full day to float there, and we've only got a few hours of daylight left. That won't work."

"What about trails?" another leader asked. "Maybe we could carry him out and go back toward where we stopped for lunch. We passed a forest service cabin along there somewhere."

"I already looked. There are no trails anywhere around here. It's all like this." He motioned to the steep bank and wildly tossing trees. The wind seemed to be letting up slightly, but it was still a constant, dull roar.

Curtis was unusually quiet. He handed Randy bandages and helped as he could, but he felt almost detached from the scene. Even the sight of his father's thickly bandaged head didn't upset him. None of it seemed real. He shivered and folded his arms in front of him. When had it started getting so cold?

"Curtis, your arm *is* bleeding! Let me see it." Mr. Miller had been standing out of the way, but now he was staring at the rivulets of blood streaking down Curtis's right arm.

Randy looked up as his brother obediently held out his arm and rolled it over, exposing the long, gaping wound left by the rock. Randy gasped. "Curt, how did that happen? I didn't know you were hurt. I thought it was just . . ."

"I'm okay." Curtis was peering down curiously at the gash on his arm. Funny, he still couldn't feel anything.

Randy stared at him, his throat tight. Whatever their disagreements in the past, Curtis was his brother. He should've noticed that he was injured.

"I think you'd better lie down," Mr. Miller told Curtis. "You're looking pale. Come back here behind this rock where it's flat and let me bandage that." He quickly led the teenager away.

"He acts like he's going into shock," Mr. Hansen told Randy once they were out of earshot. "There's no telling how much blood he's lost. It'll be better if he's up there where he can't see your father."

Randy nodded mutely. How had it happened that both his father and brother had been badly injured, yet he'd come out without a scratch? He'd been standing literally shoulder to shoulder with Curtis when the boulder came crashing down.

His father was moaning. "Those people!" he said. "Purple capes. Make them . . ." He pushed Randy violently aside and struggled into a sitting position, but it didn't last long. He vomited, then sank back down, his face white as paper.

Randy got him calmed again, then jumped up to go check on Curtis.

He didn't realize how scared he was until he took his first few steps. His legs were rubbery, his mouth dry, his stomach so knotted he could hardly breathe. He was relieved to find his brother still conscious, half-leaning against a large rock. Mr. Miller was talking to him.

"Is—is he doing okay?" Randy asked.

"Yeah, I think so. Anybody come up with a plan to get all of them to a hospital?"

"Mr. Hunter said the nearest ranch is a day downstream."

They both knew that even a few more hours would be too late for Ron Hall. They needed a miracle—or a fast jet boat. Both seemed equally unlikely to appear in this rugged wilderness in the middle of a storm.

Miracles and Jet Boats

The rain started in earnest as Randy picked his way down to check on his father. Within seconds, his face was wet and his eyes blurred and stinging.

I should just sit down and cry while I've got the chance, he thought, rubbing the back of his hand across his eyes. I don't know why I'm not already crying. There's no way

Dad's going to make it. This is all hopeless.

The crowd of leaders was knotted nearby, still trying to figure out some way to get help, when suddenly they all got quiet. "Listen!" one of them said. They turned to face the river.

Randy heard it a moment later, a distant hum gradually increasing to a roar. It was the sound of a jet boat heading their way.

"Hey!" Randy shouted. "Hey, it's a boat!" He ran down to the water's edge, no longer aware of the rain. Straining his eyes, he was the first to spot the silver jet boat as it sliced around a bend heading downriver.

Instantly the whole group started yelling and waving. The driver, wearing a baseball cap and sunglasses, at first just smiled and waved back, seeing what appeared to be an excited group of Boy Scouts jumping up and down on the riverbank. It took him a moment to realize that none of them was smiling.

Something was wrong.

He quickly turned the boat toward the shore and cut back the power, letting the craft drift in close. "How're you folks doing?" he called out.

They all shouted at once that they needed a ride back upstream, but Stan Watt shook his head politely. "Sorry, but I'm on my way to run medicine to some handicapped children at the Outfitter's Camp. I really can't stop."

"No, you don't understand!" Mr. Hunter shouted. "We've got people hurt! We have to go *now!*" He pointed to where Ron Hall, heavily bandaged, was lying on blood-stained rocks.

The jet boat driver's jaw dropped. "The kids can wait. Let's load him up!" He introduced himself as Stan Watt from Blackfoot.

"We've got another man with a broken leg who needs to go too," Mr. Hunter said. "He's in a lot of pain. John? You and your dad come get in the boat!"

"My brother is hurt, too," Randy said. "Come on, Curtis!"

In no time at all they had Mr. Hall stretched out on a bench seat in the boat with Randy on a cooler next to him, cradling his head. John Anderson helped his father get as comfortable as possible. Curtis sat near Randy.

"Everybody ready?" Mr. Watt asked. He turned the boat around in one smooth move and pointed it upstream at full throttle. Within seconds the forlorn group left on the shore was out of sight.

"How far is it to the nearest phone?" Randy shouted.

"There's a Fire Outlook Station coming up in about ten minutes," Mr. Watt shouted back. "I'm not sure if they have a phone, but I know they have a radio. They can use it to call for help."

Running against the current made for a jarring ride. Randy tried to cushion his father's head against the jolts, but it wasn't much use. In the back, Ray Anderson was grimacing in pain each time the boat rose and slammed back down. His leg was in bad shape.

"Can you make it a little less bumpy?" Randy yelled. "It's hurting these guys."

Mr. Watt shook his head. "We're fighting the current. Just hang on!"

The Fire Outlook Station was a cabin perched high on one bank. Mr. Watt pulled over and killed the engine. "I'll go up and tell them to call for a Life Flight. You guys stay put."

Randy was too impatient to sit in the boat. "I'll go. I can probably get up there faster." Easing his father's head onto the seat, he jumped onto the shore and raced up the hill.

He was out of breath by the time he reached the cabin. He ran inside and blurted out, "We need to call somebody! We need a Life Flight!" He had a hard time spitting it out.

The man at the station looked at the teenager in astonishment. "You need what?"

"A Life Flight. A helicopter. Hurry!"

"Settle down, settle down. Now why don't you tell me exactly what the problem is and let me decide what's needed, eh?"

Randy wanted to scream. "We . . . need . . . a . . . helicopter!" he said through clenched teeth. "It's an emergency. My dad and some others are hurt."

Stan Watts walked in just in time to hear the man's disbelieving response. "*Listen* to him!" he roared, which made the man jump. "Get a helicopter up here *now*. We've got two males fifty-five and above, one with severe head trauma and another with a shattered leg, and a teenage male with a severe laceration on his right arm who's showing signs of shock. If we don't get help fast we're going to need some body bags!"

The man's face turned white. He made the call. After he hung up he said, "Okay, paramedics are on their way, but you'll have to meet them at Corn Creek. They can't land a helicopter here. They should be waiting when you get there."

"Thanks," Randy said sarcastically as he and Mr. Watt ran for the door.

Down in the boat, Curtis was getting worried. Randy and the driver had been gone a long time, and his father was moaning and tossing. Blood was once again seeping through the bandages on his head.

"Dad, please stay still," Curtis pleaded, resting his good hand gently on his father's chest. "We're trying to get help for you." He still felt cold and lightheaded, like he was moving in slow motion.

His father raised a hand as if to say "wait a minute," then rolled to one side and threw up. Curtis was startled when he saw that it was almost all blood. He stared at it stupidly, trying to remember what he should do.

Then Randy and the driver returned. "We have to keep going to Corn Creek," Randy explained as the engine roared back to life. "The Life Flight will meet us there."

"Dad's vomiting blood, and his head's starting to bleed again," Curtis said. "We need to hurry."

Mr. Hall's condition was deteriorating rapidly. Randy, sitting on the ice chest and holding his father's head, suddenly realized that the seat of his pants felt soaked. His first thought was that the ice chest had leaked, but when he twisted around to look, he saw that he was sitting in a pool of blood.

Randy looked around the boat wildly. "I need a towel or T-shirt, fast! Dad's head is bleeding again really bad!" The once-white bandages on his head were completely saturated with blood.

Curtis's T-shirt was strapped down under his life jacket, and he didn't see any towels or rags inside the boat. He saw only one thing that might work. "Here, take this," he said, unwinding the thick bandage wrapped around his right arm.

Randy stared at him. "No, Curt, leave that on! Your arm is hurt."

"It's okay. Dad needs it more than I do."

Randy's throat grew tight. "Look, buddy, just leave it on. I mean it. I'll find something else." Curtis finally nodded and replaced his bandage.

Mr. Hall's breathing was becoming ragged and shallow. Randy held him tightly, willing him to hang on just a little longer. "How much farther to Corn Creek?" he yelled.

"We're almost there!" Mr. Watts eased the jet boat around the last bend, revealing a cluster of ambulances waiting onshore. As the jet boat pulled up and stopped, they all came running.

"Dad? We're here. You're gonna be okay now." Randy hoped his father could hear him. He was lying very still.

A dragonfly-like forest service helicopter darted over the

trees above them and circled overhead as the paramedics crowded onto the boat. One tapped Randy's shoulder.

"You can let go of your father now," she said gently. "We'll take it from here. You go on with the others."

"But I . . ."

"We need to get your father stabilized so we can transport him. We need room to work."

Reluctantly, Randy and Curtis followed a paramedic up the boat ramp to a small travel trailer parked nearby. "Let's step inside here where we can look at your arm," he said to Curtis.

Curtis went in, but Randy stood just outside the door where he could keep an eye on the boat. The small dragonfly copter landed in the clearing behind him, and it looked like they might be getting Mr. Anderson ready to go. Why weren't they bringing his dad up?

The *whup-whup-whup* sound of another helicopter made him look up. A Life Flight sliced overhead, then circled. The only place to land was where the forest service helicopter was, so the smaller craft took off and landed just across the river. The Life Flight set down in the clearing.

Still, nobody brought Mr. Hall up the ramp.

Randy stuck his head in the door of the trailer. The paramedic was cleaning and rebandaging Curtis's wound.

"He says I'm going to need stitches," Curtis said. "It still doesn't hurt. I can't figure that out."

They both looked outside when a woman paramedic came tearing up from the boat to grab a small box of some kind, then raced back down. She was running so fast she was almost falling down. Randy's heart thudded painfully in his chest. He looked at his brother, seeing the same fear reflected in his face.

"Do you think Dad's okay?" asked Curtis.

"I hope so. I'm going down there to see what's going on. I'll be right back."

But the paramedics wouldn't even let him get close. Kindly but firmly, they told him to go back up and stay with his brother. Randy caught only a brief glimpse of his father, an oxygen mask strapped over his pale face and electrodes attached to his chest, before turning back.

He trudged back up the ramp, torn between anger and anxiety. In front of the ranger's station he saw an old-fashioned green water pump. He looked down at his hands and clothes, which were sticky with blood. He decided to wash up and get a drink.

He was pumping the handle with one hand and trying to catch the spurts of water in the other when the ranger walked over. "Let me help. This pump doesn't work very well with just one person."

"Thanks." Randy splashed water on his face and scrubbed his hands and arms as best he could, scraping at his crusty skin with his fingernails. It was going to take a lot of water to even make a dent.

Curtis, his arm freshly bandaged, was watching the boat from the doorway of the camper. He jumped up when he saw the paramedics lifting his dad off on a stretcher. Where was Randy? He spotted him at the pump and quickly joined him.

"They're bringing Dad up," he said.

They both turned and watched in silence as the paramedics carried Mr. Hall to the helicopter and started loading him. He was strapped to the stretcher. It didn't look like he was moving. They knew this might be the last time they'd see him alive—if he *was* still alive. Nobody was telling them anything.

They were still staring at the helicopter when a woman paramedic walked up and took Curtis's arm in a firm grip. "We need you to come get in the ambulance now." She started to lead him away.

Randy trailed along behind them. "Do you know where they're taking our dad?"

"I think they said they're going to St. Patrick in Missoula."

The woman ushered Curtis into the back of the ambulance. He was quiet until she threw a thick strap across his lap and tightened it down. "Why are you doing that? I don't need to be strapped down!"

"It's to make sure you don't roll off while we're moving." She clipped an instrument to one of his fingertips.

Curtis looked up at Randy with a flicker of panic in his eyes. Randy cleared his throat. "Where are you taking him?"

"Steele Memorial."

"Can I go with him?"

"Sorry, we're not allowed to take passengers."

The Life Flight's rotors suddenly came to life and sliced slowly through the air. When Randy turned to look at it, the paramedic pulled one of the ambulance doors shut behind him, blocking his view of his brother. He found himself standing alone as his father and brother prepared to disappear in different directions.

A hard lump rose in his throat. He walked back to the ranger's station and sat on a bench about halfway between the ambulance and the helicopter. He was still sitting there when a woman from the Life Flight hurried over.

"Are you a relative of Mr. Hall's?" she asked. When Randy told her he was, she shoved several items into his hands. "Here's his wedding ring, his watch and his wallet. We had to cut his clothes off and we don't want these things to get lost."

Before he could respond, she was on her way back to the helicopter. She ducked inside, the rotors sped to a blur, and a moment later the craft rose and sped away over the treetops. Randy followed it with his eyes until it was out of sight, clutching his father's most personal possessions in one hand. The silver watch . . . Albertson's had given him after ten years, his worn leather wallet, his gold wedding band . . .

An older man dressed for a day on the river was walking a dog nearby, but he stopped when he saw the expression on Randy's face. He came over and sat on the bench next to him. The dog stretched out comfortably at his feet.

"Are you okay, son?" the man asked gently. "You look all done in."

Randy closed his fist around his father's things. "I'm . . . It's just they're taking my . . ." His voice broke, and to his embarrassment, he burst into tears. He leaned forward and buried his fingers in the dog's soft fur as he fought to get himself under control.

The man seemed not to notice. "Was that your dad in the helicopter?"

Randy nodded. "And my brother's in there," he added unevenly, looking toward the ambulance. They were almost ready to leave.

"Aren't you going?"

Randy took a deep breath, trying to steady his voice. "They won't let me. They said no passengers."

"He's your brother," the man said softly. "Go with him."

His words struck Randy like an electric shock. Without another word, he jumped up and ran to the ambulance just as they were closing the other rear door.

"I'm going with my brother whether you like it or not," he said firmly, climbing in. "Don't tell me no again."

"I want him to come!" added Curtis, clearly relieved to have him there.

The paramedics exchanged a startled look, then shrugged. The two tall, blood-encrusted teenagers looked determined. What were they supposed to do? "Find a place to sit," one said.

Randy smiled over at Curtis. When the Hall brothers joined forces, nobody else had a chance.

One Year Later . . .

"Curt, come help me out with this cooler! It feels like it's loaded with rocks." Randy was staggering as he tried to jam their old ice chest into the car. They'd only packed food for a week, but it weighed a ton.

"Got it," Curtis said as he took the other end. A thick white scar on his right arm was a permanent reminder of the previous summer's rafting trip. It had taken more than thirty-five stitches to close the six-inch gash.

As they turned back toward the house to get the tent and the last of their gear, they were both grinning. It was early summer, and they were on their way up to Redfish Lake for a week-long camping trip with Jason Hunter, Alan Hunter's son.

Their mom was letting them take her car, but as they filled it with camping gear, she looked doubtful. "It's a long way to drive," she said anxiously. "Are you sure you're going to be all right?"

"We'll be fine, Mom." Randy tossed his duffel into the back and slammed the door.

Mr. Hall walked out and put his arm around his wife's shoulders. "Listen to your mother, boys. Accidents happen, so you pay attention to what you're doing!" He smiled suddenly. "But have a good time. We'll be up there in a couple days."

Mr. Hall's road to recovery had been a long one. He had arrived at the hospital with such a badly fractured skull that it took more than nine hours of surgery and seven metal plates to piece it back together. He also had injuries to his left eye and cheekbone and a severed tendon in his left hand. The hospital staff was amazed that he had survived in that state for hours out in the wilderness.

Randy and Curtis at the Eagle
Scout Court of Honor.

But seven months later, when Randy and Curtis each stood up to receive the Boy Scouts' National Lifesaving Award for their part in their father's rescue, he had been there to applaud. "I wouldn't be here if they hadn't done what they did," he told everyone proudly.

Randy slid into the driver's seat and Curtis quickly took his place beside him. With a cheerful honk of the horn and a screech of tires, the Hall brothers left for a week of camping, swimming and exploring, once again pitting themselves against Mother Nature.

Neither of them had any doubt who would win.

Curtis and his dad.

Ray Anderson had to have part of his shattered leg bone replaced with a metal rod. His son John also received the National Lifesaving Award and earned his Eagle Scout badge with Randy and Curtis Hall.

After Ron Hall was released from the hospital, Randy returned his ring and wallet, but kept his watch because he liked it. Mr. Hall is still trying to get it back.

Would You Know What to Do . . . to Stop Severe Bleeding?

Take this quiz and find out!

1. **If someone is injured and bleeding, before taking any action (other than calling 911) you should:**
   a. take photographs of the injured person in situ (in their current position)
   b. make sure you're not also in danger of injury
   c. take steps to protect yourself from contact with their blood
   d. b and c

2. **To protect yourself from blood-related diseases, you should:**
   a. use barriers like gloves and eyeglasses, and scrub your hands thoroughly with soap afterward
   b. take extra vitamin C for at least ten days after you've had contact with blood
   c. call your local Poison Control Center for instructions
   d. all the above

3. **Along with HIV infection, which can lead to AIDS, other diseases you can contract from direct contact with infected blood or body fluids include:**
   a. hepatitis C (serious liver infection that causes permanent damage)

b. herpes (infection of skin and mucous membranes; causes blisterlike sores)

c. meningitis (severe infection of the covering of the brain and spinal cord)

d. all the above

4. **If you're assisting someone who is bleeding, you should avoid:**

a. touching your hair or face

b. lifting your hands above eye level, even with gloves on

c. breathing through your nose

d. wearing a hat (unless it's rubber, like a swim cap)

5. **The easiest way to stop bleeding from an external wound is to:**

a. apply a tourniquet above the wound, easing it frequently to keep from cutting off circulation

b. apply direct pressure and elevate the injured area

c. liberally sprinkle vitamin K powder into and around the wound

d. drape spider webs over the wound

6. **If a bandage or cloth becomes soaked through with blood:**

a. immediately replace it with a clean, dry bandage

b. remove the soaked bandage, cleanse the wound again, then replace with a clean bandage

c. do nothing; the soaked bandage will dry quickly and form a natural scab

d. leave the soaked bandage in place and stack another clean, dry bandage on top of it

7. **If you suspect a head injury that involves a skull fracture, DO NOT:**
   a. apply direct pressure to the head wound—you can do further harm by pressing bone fragments into the brain
   b. remove debris from the wound and rinse it with sterile water
   c. cover the wound
   d. a and b

8. **If someone is wearing a helmet (football helmet, motorcycle helmet, etc.) when they're injured, you should:**
   a. carefully remove the helmet to check for head injuries
   b. leave the helmet on until paramedics arrive
   c. use a chisel to chip away broken or crushed parts of the helmet so you can inspect injuries without removing it
   d. none of the above

9. **If someone is injured, but tells you they don't want your help, you should:**
   a. back off immediately
   b. insist on helping them
   c. warn them that they might die if you don't do something
   d. knock them out, then help them

10. **If someone loses a lot of blood, you should watch for signs of _____ and be prepared to act.**
    a. anemia
    b. shock
    c. hypoglycemia
    d. senility

Answers: 1-d, 2-a, 3-d, 4-a, 5-b, 6-d, 7-d, 8-b, 9-a, 10-b

Give yourself ten points for each correct answer, then check your score below:

90–100: *Teens 911 Top Gun.* You've demonstrated an unusually high level of knowledge and skills. Congratulations!
80: You've demonstrated an above-average level of knowledge and skills. Not bad.
60–70: While you've demonstrated at least some basic knowledge, it's not enough to keep you (or someone you're trying to help) out of trouble.
50 or Below: I hope you're not a Scout, because at this rate it'll take you ten years to earn your First Aid merit badge!

For More Information

Call your local Red Cross (listed in your phone book under "American Red Cross") to check into taking a first aid course. It only takes a few hours, and it can help save a life—maybe even your own.

Flameproof

When Tony realizes his house is on fire, he can save himself by jumping out the window—but can he leave his
little brother and sister inside?

Quit wiggling or you'll tip the bike!" Tony exclaimed as he balanced his kid brother, Freddie, on the handlebars in front of him. Like many native New Yorkers, sixteen-year-old Antonio "Tony" Guzman didn't own a car. He took a bus to school and work, and either walked or rode his chrome Mongoose everywhere else. He didn't mind the exercise. He was on the varsity wrestling team at Brentwood High School and had to stay in shape.

It was late afternoon as he took his eleven-year-old brother to play basketball at the park down the street. In addition to keeping Freddie's weight balanced on the handlebars, Tony had to peddle bowlegged to keep from knocking the basketball out of the bike's frame where it was wedged. He grinned at the thought of how they must look. He didn't care. With his muscular build, people rarely tried to make fun of him.

"I hear the ice cream man!" Freddie yelled suddenly,

causing the bike to wobble as he leaned forward and pointed. "He's up there by the park entrance. Hurry, Tony!"

Tony sped up. "You got any money?" he asked breathlessly. Money was tight in their family, so ice cream cones were a rare treat.

"Mommy gave me a dollar for cleaning up the living room. Hurry!"

A moment later they skidded to a stop beside the ice cream truck. Freddie jumped down and handed over his dollar for a vanilla cone, then carefully climbed back onto the handlebars. "Thanks, Tony."

"No problem, just don't drip on my bike."

They entered the park and were starting to make the loop around the six basketball courts to find an empty one when the bike hit a speed bump. The unexpected jolt sent Freddie's ice cream cone flying. With an anguished cry, the boy looked down to find his cone empty, the single scoop of ice cream splattered in the dirt.

"Tony!" he wailed, fighting back tears.

A sudden burst of laughter from the nearest basketball court caused Tony's head to whip around. The group of teenagers playing there had watched the whole thing. They were laughing at Freddie.

Tony put an arm around his brother's narrow shoulders. "Hey, don't worry about it. We can go home and get ice cream out of the freezer."

As the other boys continued to laugh and point, Tony's jaw grew tight with anger. He finally turned to face them.

"This is my brother," he said in a sharp tone. "Why don't you mind your own business and leave him alone?"

One boy said something and elbowed the others. They laughed even harder. Fists clenched, Tony started toward them when Freddie hastily grabbed his arm.

"I want to go home," Freddie said. "Can we just go?"

Tony looked down at his little brother. They both had brown eyes and dark brown, almost black hair, but Freddie was skinny where Tony was muscular. With an effort, the teenager smiled. "That's probably a real good idea. Let's go." He glanced back at the boys on the court. They weren't laughing anymore. Apparently the look on his face had warned them to stop.

The ride back home was quiet. Freddie was still upset, but determined not to cry. Tony worked off his anger by pedaling hard. He'd never liked bullies, especially when they picked on helpless younger kids, but he was glad Freddie had stopped him. Fighting was dumb unless he was competing for a medal.

They reached the house and rode around to the back yard. The Guzmans lived in a two-story ranch house that was divided into two apartments. They rented the ground floor, and their aunt, uncle and cousins rented the upper floor. The Guzman's "front door" was actually in the back.

"Come on," Tony said, ushering Freddie up the concrete steps to the door. "I'll make a little bowl of ice cream and bring it to you, okay?"

"Mommy won't let me have ice cream this close to dinner," Freddie protested.

Tony smiled. "She'll think it's for me. She knows I eat all the time!" Freddie's face brightened, and he obediently headed for his room.

The kitchen and living room were combined into one large area with the kitchen nearest the door and the bedrooms down a hall off to the left. Tony was opening cabinets looking for a bowl when Monica Guzman emerged from the hall, two-year-old Priscilla at her heels.

"Hi," Tony said, waving a spoon at his mother. "Hi Priscilla. What'cha up to?"

"Yony!" Priscilla said with glee, trotting over on chubby legs to wrap her arms around his knees. Grinning, Tony set the bowl and spoon aside long enough to pry her off his legs and toss her up in the air a couple times. She squealed happily, her dark eyes sparkling.

"Eating again," Mrs. Guzman said with mock resignation. "You'll eat us out of house and home if you keep that up."

"Gotta keep up my strength," Tony replied, flexing a bulging bicep.

Mrs. Guzman just made a shooing motion with her hand. Taking the hint, Tony sauntered off down the hall to deliver the ice cream to Freddie.

Fight to the Finish

The main hall at Brentwood High School was crowded and noisy as Tony pushed his way through to his locker. Even though he was a lowly freshman, he was greeted with smiles and slaps on the back. His performance on the

Tony Guzman with his parents, Priscilla, Freddie and other family members.

school's varsity wrestling team had already gained a lot of attention.

It was Friday. That afternoon he'd be traveling with his team to the North Babylon High School tournament, but since he wasn't scheduled to compete he'd enjoyed a big dinner the night before and a hearty breakfast that morning. He was eight pounds over his fighting weight of 145.

He slammed his locker and was on his way to his first period class when head coach Bob Penorello spotted him and called out, "Tony, wait!"

"Hey Coach," Tony greeted him. "What's up?"

"You got first seat," Coach Penorello replied without preamble. "Congratulations, you're wrestling this afternoon."

He eyed Tony's solid midsection with a frown. "What's your weight?"

"Uh, I'm probably five pounds over," Tony replied, smacking his stomach with his palm. "I didn't know I was wrestling today. Really, first-seated! That's great!" Wrestlers were ranked by "seats," with first seat going to the most skilled. It meant Tony would be fighting his first match early in the tournament.

"Five pounds? That's not good. If it was just a couple pounds you could sweat it off today, but . . . "

"I can do it, Coach! I'll make my weight before the tournament. Give me a chance."

"Well, you've got"—Coach Penorello glanced at his watch—"about seven hours to lose those five pounds. See if you can get excused from your classes today and hit the gym."

"No doubt. Thanks, Coach!"

Tony quickly made the rounds to get permission from each teacher to miss class. Since it was Friday and he had no major tests, they all said he could go. He crammed his books back into his locker, grabbed his gym bag, and headed for the locker room.

Coach would have a fit if he knew I was eight pounds over, Tony thought as he stepped onto the scale. He halfway hoped several of the pounds had mysteriously vanished on the way to school.

They hadn't.

From past experience, Tony knew that he could lose two or three pounds with a hard calorie-burning workout and another couple pounds of water weight by sweating it off. But *eight* pounds?

I guess I should've skipped thirds at dinner last night, he thought ruefully.

He pulled on a rubber workout suit to trap his body heat, then added a couple more layers of clothes. After a moment's thought, he dragged a stationary bike into the shower room and went around turning on showers. Within a couple minutes the room was filled with steam.

Here we go, Tony thought as he climbed on the bike, positioned his feet and started pedaling. At least I don't have to balance Freddie on the handlebars this time!

Three hours later, after switching off between the stationary bike and jumping rope in the makeshift "steam room," Tony tossed aside his soggy sweat suit, peeled off the rubber suit, and walked wearily to the scale. To his dismay Coach Newell picked that moment to check on his progress.

"How's it going?" the coach asked, stepping behind Tony to read the scale. "I hear you came in five over this morning." There was no way to block his view since it was an upright doctor's scale. Tony held his breath as he slid the lower weight to the one hundred–pound mark, then slid the upper weight to 145 . . . 146 . . . 147 . . . 148 . . . Tony glanced over his shoulder as he continued to nudge the weight up the scale. One hundred and forty-nine . . . 150. The scale finally steadied out. He'd lost three pounds!

"Still one-fifty?" Coach Newell exclaimed. "I thought you told Coach Penorello that you were only five over! What'd you eat for dinner last night?"

Tony grinned sheepishly. "Ice, Coach! Just ice! I don't know where all this weight came from."

"Uh-huh. Well, you've got another four hours to lose five more pounds. Are you sure you can do this without hurting yourself?"

"Yeah, yeah, don't worry about it! I'm just getting started." Tony ran his fingers through his sweat-soaked hair. No way was he going to miss out on a chance to compete in the tournament, even if it meant jumping rope all the way over to North Babylon High.

By the time school ended at three o'clock, Tony had worked his way down to 145½—still half a pound over. His legs felt like lead as he climbed the steps into the school bus to join his team.

"I'm so tired I don't know how I'm going to wrestle," he moaned as he sank into a seat. "I've never worked out this hard in my life!"

His teammates all nodded in sympathy. In wrestling matches, weight was critical. Even half a pound could get you disqualified.

During the twenty-minute drive to the other school, Tony kept hoping for a miracle. Maybe North Babylon's scale would be half a pound under! Or maybe Brentwood's scale was half a pound over. In either case he'd make the weight.

When he stepped on the scale a few minutes later, though, the miracle didn't happen. He was still over. He groaned.

Tony's long-time coach from junior high was there

assisting the Brentwood coaches. Ralph Naplatano, "Coach Nap" to the team, shook his head sympathetically.

"You've still got an hour," he said. "That's when you'll be up for your first match. Why don't you go run or something? Maybe you can still do it."

Tony was so tired he could hardly stand, but he couldn't let his teammates down. "Right," he said. Taking a deep breath, he jogged to the edge of the gym and started running laps.

An hour later, soaked with sweat, legs aching with exhaustion, Tony was called to weigh in. He stepped onto the scale and froze, afraid to look as the coach moved first one weight, then the other.

"You did it!" Coach Nap exclaimed, slapping him on the back. "You're just under one forty-five. Get ready to wrestle!"

Relief made Tony feel almost more weary. He asked, "Who am I matched with?"

"Somebody from Deer Park," Coach Nap replied. "Remember, this will be your easiest match. If you win you'll get a chance to rest for a couple hours before you're up again."

The mats were ready in the center of the gym. A large colored circle defined the outside boundary, and a smaller circle in the middle showed where the two opponents would start each match. Unlike boxing rings, wrestling rings aren't roped off.

When Tony's name was called, he stepped onto the mat and walked to the center ring. His opponent from Deer

Park stepped up. They stood facing each other, careful to keep their feet behind the taped lines that marked their starting positions.

He's bigger than me, Tony thought with a sinking heart. The fact was, almost everybody there was bigger. As a freshman, Tony was younger than most of the others. He'd only competed in one high school tournament, and in that one, he'd been eliminated in the first round.

The referee joined them in the small circle. At his nod, Tony reached forward to shake his opponent's hand. The match would last six minutes, unless one of them pinned the other first, throwing him flat on his back with both shoulder blades to the mat, and holding him in that position for at least a couple seconds. Otherwise it would be fought in three periods: three minutes, one and one-half minutes, one and one-half minutes.

The referee stepped back and blew his whistle, signaling the start of the match. Tony lunged forward.

His first move was an overhook, which successfully threw his opponent to the mat. The Deer Park wrestler instantly rolled from his back to his stomach and came up fighting. From that point, Tony was too focused on his moves to remember how tired he was.

He was almost surprised a few minutes later to find himself straddling his opponent, holding him flat against the mat until the referee blew his whistle. It was a pin. He had won the match!

"Yes!" Tony exclaimed with jubilation. With a sudden burst of energy he jumped to his feet and shook his opponent's hand. As their hands clasped, the referee stepped forward to grip each wrestler's wrist with one hand, then he lifted Tony's hand high in the air.

Tony grinned as his coaches and teammates clapped and cheered.

"You thought I was going to lose, didn't you?" he asked laughingly as he joined his teammates. "You know what they say, the bigger they are the harder they fall!"

Coach Nap slapped him on the back proudly. "You've come a long way from that little junior high kid I started with," he said. "Good job, Tony."

Coach Penorello echoed the congratulations. "You've got some time to relax, so get something to eat and drink before your next match!"

All the wrestlers knew that once they made their weight at the beginning of the tournament, they wouldn't be weighed again that day. It wasn't unusual for them to add on two to four pounds between matches by chugging water and eating a small meal. Even a couple pounds could give them a slight advantage against a lighter opponent.

After his grueling day Tony spent the next two hours resting. When his name was called for the next round, he jumped to his feet with confidence. After battling all day to make his weight and winning the first round, there was no way he was going to lose now.

It was a tougher fight this time, but Tony once again came out on top. He rejoined his teammates and watched as the other weight classes competed. It was close to eleven o'clock that night before the day's matches were completed. As the Brentwood team climbed back on the school bus, Coach Nap asked Tony if he needed a ride home from the school.

"Yeah, I guess I do," Tony replied. "I think I've missed the last bus."

"I'll drop you off on my way home. I want you to get a good night's sleep so you'll be ready in the morning." The coach checked his schedule. "It looks like you'll be fighting North Babylon first thing."

The house was quiet when Tony walked in, but he could hear the television in the living room. His mother and Freddie were still up. As usual, Tony's first stop was the refrigerator.

"So how'd you do?" called Mrs. Guzman.

Tony was peering around inside the refrigerator, trying to decide how much he could eat. On the second day of a tournament they were allowed an extra two pounds, but he didn't want to go through all the work to make his weight again. He was pretty sure he'd already gained back at least two pounds since the weigh-in.

"I won both matches today," he answered nonchalantly. "Tomorrow I'll advance to the finals if I win my first match."

"That's good," his mother said. Freddie bounced up and ran into the kitchen. "So who'd you beat? Was it hard?"

Tony laughed and ruffled Freddie's hair. "I didn't know either of them, but they were both bigger than me. I didn't think I could do it, especially the first match. I was so tired I could hardly move."

He went on to tell how he'd slaved all day to lose eight pounds. He made a joke out of it all for Freddie, describing how the coach had asked what he'd eaten for dinner the night before.

"And so I said, 'Ice, Coach! Just ice!' I don't think he believed me."

Freddie howled with laughter, and across the room Mrs. Guzman smiled. "That'll be the day."

The next morning Tony won his match against North Babylon, but not without difficulty. In tournaments, each new round was set up to be harder than the last. Tony's final match would be the toughest of all.

"You're up against Freeport in the finals," Coach Penorello told him. "This other kid's heavier and stronger than you, but you can still beat him. Just keep your focus."

"I'll do my best," Tony assured him.

When the match was called, Tony stepped up, shook his opponent's hand and waited with a pounding heart for the whistle. He wanted so bad to take home a medal!

The whistle blew. Cheers echoed through the gym as the two teens locked in their first hold, each trying to toss the other to the mat. There was no easy pin this time in the first three-minute period, and Tony was out of breath when the ref blew his whistle to signal a break.

"You're doing fine," Coach Nap said. "You're about even on points so far. Just watch yourself."

"Right," Tony said breathlessly. A minute later the whistle blew to signal the start of the second period. They had one and one-half minutes this time.

Despite the other teen's size advantage, Tony managed to hold his own. When the second period ended, they were still even in points. It was going to be a very close match.

Tony wiped the sweat from his face and prepared for the final one and one-half minute period. The next ninety seconds would determine which of them would receive the medal.

The excitement in the gym rose as the whistle blew. The Freeport wrestler locked Tony with an underhook and lifted him easily off his feet, pushing him toward the out of bounds circle. With just seconds left on the clock, Tony was down by one point. One point, like one pound, was all it took to lose your chance in a wrestling tournament.

I can't come this close and then quit, thought Tony as he grappled for a hold. I've got to do it. I've got to!

His determination renewed, Tony decided to use a drop step to try to sweep his opponent's legs out from under him. Even if he couldn't pin him—hardly likely at this point—he might gain a small point advantage that would let him take the match.

With the familiarity of long practice, he quickly positioned himself for the move: feet planted about shoulder width apart, right foot slightly ahead, knees bent, body lowered almost into a crouch, right shoulder rolled down and forward. In a lightning fast move, he shot forward and made solid contact with his opponent's legs, lifted—and flipped him over onto his back!

Tony could hardly believe it. He pounced, holding the

other teen flat against the mat for an instant until the whistle blew.

It was a pin. He'd won!

With his hand held aloft by the ref, Tony resisted the impulse to jump up and down and show off. The coaches had drilled it onto all of them to accept both victory and defeat with grace. "You shouldn't act surprised when you win," Coach Nap had advised him. "Act like you expected it all along!"

Tony managed to stay cool until he walked off the mat to join his teammates. "I can't believe this," he said as they surrounded him, hugging him and slapping his back. "I really didn't think I could do it."

At the end of the day, after the last match was fought, it was time for the awards ceremony. Each weight group was called up one at a time, and the wrestlers lined up in winning order. When it was Tony's turn to step up on the platform, he walked over to stand in first place. Coach Penorello presented the first place medal, slipping it over Tony's head so it hung around his neck.

"Congratulations, Tony," he said. "You earned it today."

Tony stared down at the heavy medallion resting on his chest. It was nothing like the cheap junior high medals he'd won. This one was huge, a heavy gold medallion with two wrestlers embossed on it. Even the blue and white ribbon was thicker.

Against all odds, he'd done it. He grinned, his teeth gleaming white against his dark complexion. He couldn't wait to show his family.

A Different Kind of Medal

Tony wandered through the flea market, keeping his cousin Melissa company as she browsed. He swung his arms to loosen them up, then laughed at himself. Usually when he was at the flea market in Queens, he was tired from unloading trucks, his weekend job during the summer. During the week, he worked as a summer camp counselor, teaching and entertaining groups of young kids. He wasn't sure which job was the hardest.

"Let's go down here," Melissa said, waving toward a large booth. She was tall and thin with long dark hair. Tony followed, already bored. People brought some really weird stuff to sell.

They stopped at a stall that had everything from food to furniture. While Melissa tried on a pair of earrings, Tony fingered some other heavy chains. One necklace with a medallion caught his eye. He picked it up, letting it dangle down from his fingers. It was a Superman medallion!

Tony laughed. "How much is this?" He didn't usually spend his hard-earned paycheck on junk, but it would be fun to wear the medallion with the large S.

The vendor shrugged. "You can have it for fifteen dollars."

"Nah, that's too much. How about five?"

They went back and forth for a few minutes until they finally agreed on ten dollars. Tony handed over the money and slipped the chain over his head so the S rested in the center of his chest. If he couldn't wear his wrestling medals, he thought with amusement, he might as well be Superman.

"How do I look?" he asked Melissa, striking a Supermanly pose.

She smiled and rolled her eyes. "Give it up, Tony!"

The following week Tony wore the medallion to camp. "Not all kids have Superman as their counselor," he joked as the kids fingered the heavy metal S. They followed him around like ducklings, asking questions and hanging all over him, but he didn't mind. He was used to Freddie and Priscilla following him around at home. It was part of being a big brother.

The summer camp was staffed by many teachers off for the summer. This year, Coach Penorello was running the camp, which made him Tony's boss. It turned out to be convenient when Tony had to request his first day off.

"Hey Coach," he said during a break between classes. "Coach Nap is getting married next Friday, and I'd really like to go to his wedding if I can. Is it okay if I take that day off?"

"I don't think that'll be a problem," Coach Penorello replied. "Tell Ralph I said congratulations!"

"I will," Tony said gratefully. He felt a little guilty for skipping out on work like that, but he really liked Coach Nap. Besides, it would be funny to see him in a tuxedo instead of gym clothes!

An Odd Glow

Tony's eyes popped open. He rolled sideways to peer sleepily at the silent alarm clock by his bed, then sat up in a hurry. It was already 7 A.M. He was late! He was out of bed and halfway across the room before he remembered that it was Friday, Coach Nap's wedding day. He didn't have to go anywhere for hours and hours.

"Oh man!" he muttered to himself. "The one day I can sleep in and I wake up anyway." He yawned and scratched his chest, smiling when he realized he'd worn his Superman medallion to bed. Great outfit—boxers and a fake silver necklace!

He could hear his mom stirring around the kitchen, getting ready for work, and since he was already up he decided to say hi before she left. His dad had already left before dawn for his warehouse job.

"I didn't expect to see you up this morning!" Mrs. Guzman said in surprise when Tony yawned his way into the kitchen. "Don't you have the day off from work?"

"Yeah, but I woke up anyway, can you believe it?" Tony poured himself a glass of water and chugged it. "I'm going to back to bed, but I wanted to tell you bye first."

Mrs. Guzman smiled. "That's nice. Now don't forget to send Freddie and Priscilla upstairs to your aunt's apartment before you leave for the wedding. They're both still asleep."

"Got it. I'm going back to bed. Take it easy."

"I wish!" Mrs. Guzman replied wryly. "They don't pay me to take it easy."

Tony walked back to his room feeling lucky. I get to sleeeeep, he thought happily, drawing out the word in his mind like a lazy stretch. The wedding wasn't until after noon, so he could sleep all morning if he felt like it. Too bad he didn't have more coaches getting married.

Minutes after his head hit the pillow, he was out.

Something woke him up hours later, but this time he came around more slowly. His mouth was dry and he felt confused, almost drugged. Had he been dreaming something strange?

He slitted his eyes, trying to see what time it was, then frowned. An odd pinkish glow filled his room. What in the world was that? Then an acrid smell hit his nostrils. Something was burning.

Tony's first thought was that his brother was cooking, or trying to. I'm going to kill the kid, he thought angrily. The one day I can sleep in and he messes around with the stove! He jumped up, his bare feet hitting the floor with a thump.

"Freddie!" he bellowed. "What do you think you're doing?" Crossing his room in a couple quick steps he jerked open the door, intending to storm down the hall into the kitchen. Instead, a huge cloud of hot, black smoke hit him squarely in the face and billowed past him into the room. It forced him back. Gasping, eyes stinging, Tony staggered backwards and slammed the door.

The house was on fire, and his little brother and sister were asleep inside.

Lost in Black Smoke

Tony's chest heaved as he tried to catch his breath. Smoke or not, he had to get to Freddie and Priscilla. He sucked in a huge breath of smoky air and tried once again to get into the hall, but it was too much. Not only could he not stop coughing, he couldn't see. It was like stepping into total darkness.

He retreated again, slamming the door in frustration. "I've got to do something!" he yelled. He raced to the window and flung it open, intending to take a breath of fresh air before trying again to make it down the hallway, but as he leaned out he realized he'd never make it. The hallway was already too far gone.

"Forget this!" he said aloud. Like lightning he climbed onto the windowsill and jumped out, clearing the two bushes under his window. He landed on his feet and turned to race toward the front door.

Just then his cousins, Chico and George, came running around the corner of the house. "Hey, your house is on fire!" Chico shouted. At any other time his statement of the obvious would've been funny, but there was no time for joking.

"I know," Tony said shortly. "Freddie and Priscilla are still in there! I'm going in through the front door. Go call nine-one-one!"

Still barefoot and wearing only boxers, Tony ran up the couple of concrete steps to the door and grabbed the doorknob. It was too hot to hold for more than a second.

Thinking quickly, he ran to grab a shirt off the clothesline in the yard. Maybe he could use it to keep his hand from getting burned.

George was trying to break down the door by kicking at it, but he wasn't budging it. Tony shoved him aside and reached for the doorknob again. He was startled to feel it being turned from the other side.

"Tony!" He heard Freddie's panicked voice inside. He was trying to unlock the door!

"Freddie!" he screamed. "Open the door! Hurry up!"

The younger boy was coughing, his voice high with panic. "I'm trying!"

Tony watched helplessly from the outside as his brother struggled to turn the various locks and deadbolts in the right direction to open them. Even on normal days it could be confusing.

"Tony, I can't!" Freddie's voice was weak and shaking. He broke off into a choking cough.

Tony stared at the solid door lined with sturdy locks. His only chance was to break it down. Almost automatically he stepped back and went into a crouched drop-step position: legs staggered, knees bent, right shoulder dropped.

"Freddie! Stand away from the door!" he yelled—then charged.

His right shoulder slammed the door with great force, but the locks and hinges held. Screaming with frustration, Tony stepped back and positioned himself again. Inside, Freddie had gone silent.

With a wordless yell, he charged at the door again.

Under his determined onslaught the hinges broke and the
door splintered, falling inward at a crazy tilt. Tony fell on
top of it, landing on his hands and knees. Black smoke
belched out into the air.

As Tony picked himself up, George ran past him into
the house—then ran right back out again. "You can't go in
there!" George exclaimed. "It's hot and pitch black. You
can't see *anything!*"

Tony didn't bother to answer. He half-climbed in, over
the broken door, and plunged into the smoke calling,
"Freddie! Priscilla!" His brother had been right there at
the door just a minute before. Where was he?

By the time Tony had taken four steps into the house, he
was completely blind. Although it was broad daylight outside, the dense black smoke made it impossible for him to
see even his own outstretched hands. When he finally
took a breath it was like trying to breathe hot syrup. He
choked and gagged, his lungs straining. He barely managed to find his way back outside.

He leaned forward, propping his hands on his knees
and letting his head hang. Thoughts swirled like smoke
through his mind. How long had it been since they'd last
heard Freddie's voice? Where was Priscilla? How could
he possibly find them in that dark nightmare, much less
bring them safely back out? It was impossible!

Well then, he'd have to do the impossible.

Before George and Chico could stop him, Tony took a
big breath and ran back in, aiming for the living room.
Blinking rapidly against the stinging smoke, he turned his

face blindly one way then the other, hoping to spot Freddie or Priscilla. It was hopeless. He would have to feel his way to them.

He took a tentative step forward, arms outstretched, when Priscilla suddenly appeared in the smoke right in front of him. It was like a conjurer's trick. Before she could disappear again Tony grabbed her and shoved her small face into his shoulder. He had to get her out fast!

He turned to go back the way he came—only in the roiling smoke he couldn't tell which way led back to the door. After a panicky moment, he realized that the smoke was brushing across his face in one direction. Remembering the smoke spilling out the door, he thought it was probably going that way. He held his sister's squirming figure tight with one arm and used the other to feel his way as he followed the smoke.

After what seemed like forever he finally burst into dazzling sunlight. He drew deep, whooping breaths as he set his tiny sister down and motioned for his cousins to take her. Her face and clothes were smudged with soot and her dark eyes wide, but otherwise she looked like she'd be okay.

Tony turned back to the house. "Freddie!" he yelled, hoping against hope that the younger boy would hear his voice and follow it to safety. "Freddie, can you hear me?"

No response. If his brother was already dead, it would be insane to walk back into that searing hot nightmare. But it was his *brother*. He couldn't live with the idea of giving up on Freddie. Before he could think about it any more, he took a deep breath and ran in for the third time.

The smoke swallowed him within two steps. He quickly felt his way along the walls into the living room, thinking Freddie might have tried to go back for Priscilla. He had no breath to yell with, no way to see anything. The air was so hot that he could almost feel the skin on his bare chest and legs blistering. It all seemed unreal, like a dream.

Only you can't get hurt in your dreams, Tony thought in despair as his lungs began to ache. In dreams you can do anything. This is no dream.

He continued to walk blindly, feeling his way through the living room toward the hallway. He walked up on the fire before he even noticed it. Huge flames were leaping up from the floor almost to his face, but the air around him was already so hot that he couldn't feel the difference. He took a quick step back and hit his head against some overhead cabinets.

He was running out of time. His lungs were ready to burst. In another few seconds he would have to take a breath, and then it would be all over.

Out of nowhere, Freddie bumped into him.

Startled, relieved, Tony grabbed the younger boy's arm. Freddie was coughing and gagging but the roar of the fire had drowned it all out. Tony couldn't see his brother's face through the smoke, but he could feel his movements. He started dragging him toward the door.

In the swirling smoke it was easy to get turned around. Tony began to panic when he couldn't find the door. What if they were moving away from the door, farther into the house?

Please, Jesus, help me out here, he cried silently. *Me and my brother found each other. Help me find the way out!*

A moment later he saw a faint glimmer of light, then he was stumbling out the door and down the steps, dragging Freddie with him.

Thank God, he thought with relief. *Thank you, God.*

Even though they were out of the house, Tony didn't stop moving. His eyes were stinging too badly from the smoke to see clearly. He kept going, planning to take Freddie around to the front of the house where he thought it would be safer. For all he knew, the whole place could blow up!

As they started across the yard, though, Freddie pulled away and sank down, burying his face in the grass. Tony rubbed his burning eyes and said sharply, "Come on, Freddie, stop playing around! Get up!"

Freddie answered in a low mumble. "I'm not playing." As Tony watched in horror, Freddie started coughing up huge black chunks, his thin shoulders heaving. Tony kneeled beside him and rubbed his back helplessly. What else could he do?

Priscilla ran over and Tony put his arm around her. She was too little to understand what had happened. She looked puzzled rather than scared as she watched Freddie fight for breath.

"G'up, Freddie," she said, mimicking Tony's earlier command.

Eventually Freddie's violent coughing quieted and he

half sat up. Tony was startled when he caught his first glimpse of his brother's face. It was streaked with black, and his nostrils were caked with soot. When he opened his mouth even his teeth were black.

Priscilla giggled. "You need to brush your teef!" she lisped.

"Come on, Freddie, let me help you up," Tony said, bending close so Freddie could put an arm around his shoulders. George and Chico hovered nearby. Priscilla tried to wedge her way in to help. Once Freddie was on his feet they all started toward the front again.

They slowly made their way around the house and across the street where they sat on the curb to wait for the fire department. By the time the fire truck and ambulance came wailing down the street, the whole house was in flames. Tony watched it silently, too numb to even think about all the things they were losing. Family pictures, favorite clothes, his wrestling medals . . . everything they owned was going up in smoke.

Then he glanced down at Freddie and Priscilla. Not everything, he corrected himself. I've got all the important things right here.

When the ambulance pulled up at Southside Hospital in Bay Shore, Freddie was whisked away to be treated for smoke inhalation. Priscilla seemed fine, but the doctors wanted to check her out just in case. Tony, wearing only boxers and his Superman medallion, suddenly found himself standing alone.

"Let me get you some scrubs to put on," a nurse said.

"They're not fancy, but they're better than nothing!"

Tony accepted the blue scrubs and little booties for his feet gratefully. The bottoms of both feet were burned from stepping on the hot tiles on the kitchen floor.

"Is there somewhere I can wash up before I put these on?" he asked, looking down at his soot-streaked arms and legs. The nurse nodded and gave him directions to a nearby bathroom.

He was startled when he saw his reflection in the bathroom mirror. His eyes were red-rimmed and soot ran down his cheeks like tears. His nose was black, his nose hairs singed. He bared his teeth and saw they were also outlined in black. It would take a lot of scrubbing in the small sink to clean up all that!

It wasn't until he lifted the medallion to rinse himself off that he saw the black S imprinted on his chest. In the intense heat and smoke, the Superman medallion had left its mark.

Super Brother

"It was him! He did it!"

The chorus of voices caught Tony by surprise as he got out of the car in front of his house—or what used to be his house. The group of reporters huddled in the yard immediately trotted toward him. Most were carrying notepads. A few had cameras.

Tony was still wearing hospital scrubs. His first thought was that somebody was claiming he had started the fire.

"I didn't do it!" he said sincerely, raising his hands in surrender. "Whatever it is, I didn't do it!"

A *Newsday* reporter stepped forward. "I understand you saved your little brother and sister today. I'd just like to ask you a few questions about that."

Tony released his breath slowly. "Oh," he said in relief.

The reporter laughed. He took notes as Tony explained what had happened, then his eyes fell to the Superman medallion. "So," he said, "are you a hero like Superman?"

Tony was embarrassed. "Nah, I'm no hero. I just had to get my brother and sister out of there. Anybody with a brother and sister would've done the same thing."

The reporter raised an eyebrow. "I don't know about that. I think you must be some kind of Super-Brother to have broken down the door and made it back out of there alive!"

Tony grinned and admitted modestly, "Yeah, maybe so."

The fire was eventually found to have been caused by an electrical short. The smoke alarms in the Guzman's rental home never went off and were later found to be defective.

The Guzmans lost everything they owned in the fire, including Tony's wrestling medals and all their family photographs. The photo printed with this story is the only one they have left from that time.

Tony Guzman was awarded a plaque for his heroism.

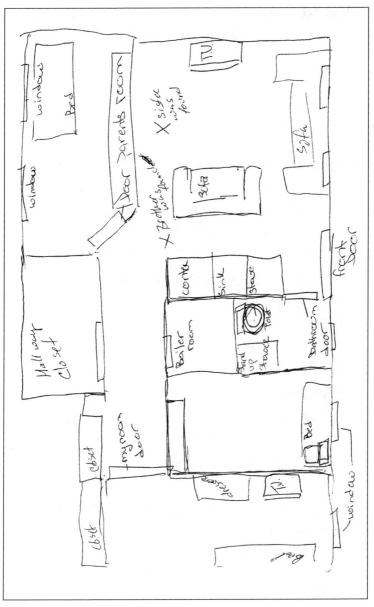

Here, Tony shows the escape route.

Would You Know How to Survive . . .
a House Fire?

Take this quiz and find out!

1. **Most deadly house fires start between the hours of:**
   a. noon and two o'clock in the afternoon
   b. five and seven o'clock at night
   c. eight and ten o'clock at night
   d. two and four o'clock in the morning

2. **Always sleep with bedroom or hall doors:**
   a. wide open
   b. tightly closed
   c. cracked about 2"
   d. cracked about 12"

3. **If you are awakened by a smoke alarm or fire:**
   a. don't panic
   b. don't stand up—drop to the floor
   c. don't take time to get dressed
   d. all of the above

4. **In a house fire, the temperature six feet off the floor can be:**
   a. 600 degrees
   b. 500 degrees
   c. 400 degrees
   d. 300 degrees

5. **If a door feels cool and safe, open it:**
    a. using a cloth to protect your hand
    b. quickly, then jump back in case smoke or heat rushes in
    c. cautiously, keeping your face to one side to avoid breathing smoke
    d. a and b

6. **If a fire occurs in the same room with you, you should:**
    a. stop, drop and roll
    b. jump out the window
    c. cover your mouth and nose with a cloth
    d. close the door behind you on the way out

7. **The average time you'll have before you succumb to smoke inhalation in a smoke-filled room is:**
    a. one or two minutes
    b. three or four minutes
    c. five or six minutes
    d. seven or eight minutes

8. **If your door feels hot, or smoke is coming through the cracks:**
    a. leave the door closed and seal the bottom crack with cloths
    b. call 911 and wait near a window for the fire department, or try to attract a neighbor's attention by yelling or waving
    c. open the door a crack to check the heat level
    d. a and b

9. **If you are forced by flames to jump from an upper window, you should:**
   a. drop pillows, blankets or other soft items to the ground to break your fall
   b. grab the corners of a bedsheet or blanket so you can "parachute" down
   c. crawl out feet-first and backwards, and lower yourself to the full length of your arms before letting go.
   d. a and c

10. **If you are able to leave an area that is on fire, you should:**
    a. find a fire extinguisher and go back to put it out
    b. close all doors between you and the fire to deprive it of oxygen and slow its spread
    c. call 911 from another room in the house
    d. set a "backfire" to limit the area that will be burned

11. **Some of the factors that make it very difficult to escape from a burning house are:**
    a. the thick, black smoke leaves you virtually blind and often disoriented
    b. the need to crawl low under the smoke slows you down
    c. the toxic (poison) smoke quickly makes you dizzy, triggers violent coughing, or leaves you unconscious
    d. all the above

12. **Unless you're actually on fire, a safety saying that can be more useful than "stop, drop and roll" is:**
    a. "If You See Sparks, Hide in the Dark"
    b. "Jump Out the Winder or You'll be a Cinder"
    c. "Fall and Crawl"
    d. "Where There's Smoke, There's Fire"

13. **A good fire safety saying to teach young brothers or sisters would be:**
    a. "Scream, Shout, and Run About"
    b. "Don't Hide. Go Outside"
    c. "Don't Cry or You'll Fry"
    d. "Red Sky at Night, Sailor's Delight"

14. **If you don't think you could abandon your family in a house fire, you should:**
    a. put together a family fire-escape plan and practice it NOW
    b. move out
    c. buy an asbestos suit and respirator
    d. find a family you don't like as much

15. **Your family's fire plan should include:**
    a. fire extinguishers in each bedroom
    b. at least one practice session jumping out of windows each month, preferably at night
    c. regular smoke alarm tests, two alternate escape routes, a meeting place outside and frequent real-time drills
    d. a bag of marshmallows and some sticks

Answers: 1-d, 2-b, 3-d, 4-a, 5-c, 6-d, 7-a, 8-d, 9-d, 10-b, 11-d, 12-c, 13-b, 14-a, 15-c

Give yourself five points for each correct answer, then see the chart below:

70–75: *Teens 911 Top Gun.* You've demonstrated an unusually high level of knowledge and skills. Congratulations!
60–65: You've demonstrated an above-average level of knowledge and skills. Not bad.
50–55: While you've demonstrated at least some basic knowledge, it's not enough to keep you (or someone you're trying to help) out of trouble.
45 or Below: Perhaps you should talk to your parents about installing a sprinkler system in your house.

Free Fire Stuff

1. Call your local Red Cross (listed in your phone book under "American Red Cross") and ask for their "Fire" checklist: ARC 4456.
2. Call the United States Fire Administration toll-free at 1-800-561-3356 and request their handout: "Escape from Fire—Once You Are Out, Stay Out!"

Race to the Finish

Jamie Chavez is a rodeo barrel racer, but she faces the most important race of her life when she finds a teacher in cardiac arrest.

It was a hot and dusty day in Bosque Farms, New Mexico, a small town just south of Albuquerque. Jamie straightened her hat and forced herself to stay relaxed in the saddle as she waited for her name to be called. As the fifteen-year-old daughter of two state rodeo champions, she had a lot to live up to.

"Jamie van Buskirk, in the hole!"

Jamie had a sudden, urgent need to go to the bathroom. She always did when she was "in the hole"—the third person in line waiting to compete. She tried to think about something else, but her mind drew a blank. In the next few minutes she and her horse would pound into the arena together and try to win the Bosque Farms High School Rodeo barrel-racing competition while a million people watched.

Well, not really a million, Jamie thought as she glanced out at the several dozen spectators. Most of them were friends and family of the competitors. She picked out her

153

mom in the crowd and felt a little better. Her mom had once
won the New Mexico State Barrel-Racing Championship
and knew exactly what Jamie was going through.

"Jamie van Buskirk, on the deck!"

Jamie's mouth went dry. Only one person left in front of
her. She drew several deep, slow breaths, then leaned forward to give Bunky a quick pat on the neck. "I'm counting on you, Bunk," she murmured "Don't be a puke with
me, okay?"

Bunky rolled an eye back at her and tossed his head
impatiently. Jamie and her mom had spent months legging
him up and getting him in shape for the season. He was
an experienced barrel horse, but he was also twenty years
old and crabby. Many of her competitors were riding
$20,000, trained barrel horses.

"Jamie van Buskirk, up next!"

Jamie working Bunky.

Time to go. Jamie leaned forward and gave Bunky a decisive kick. He reacted immediately, rearing back on his powerful hind legs as they entered the gate, then shooting forward into the arena. They hit the ground at a dead run.

Jamie pointed him toward the first barrel and urged him on, directing him with light pressure from her knees and the reins. The crowd blurred as she focused. Somewhere, she knew, an electric eye was timing her performance down to a fraction of a second. The top competitors usually came within one-tenth of a second of each other.

"Whoa, Bunk!" she snapped. She heard a faint echo of her command and realized her mom was standing at the fence nearby, backing her up with a verbal cue.

Bunky had been trained to respond to voice commands, and "whoa" meant it was time for him to turn the barrel. Like the professional he was, he cut around the three barrels with precision, leaving all of them standing. It was a perfect pattern.

Jamie's heart soared with pride as she rode back out of the arena. She sought out her mother's face and smiled. All those months of hard work and practice hadn't been in vain. She was almost positive that she and Bunky had made one of the top runs.

She waited impatiently to hear her time announced. To win, she needed to not only complete the course, but do it in the shortest time. The barrel pattern shouldn't have taken more than fifteen or sixteen seconds.

Finally the speaker crackled and the announcer spoke: "Jamie's time: sixteen-point-five seconds."

Jamie froze, the confident smile on her face slowly fading. She was nearly a full second behind the best run!

She quickly shook off the disappointment and slid off Bunky. What did she expect, competing on a twenty-year-old horse? At least he hadn't disgraced her by flipping over backwards like one of their other horses had done when she cinched him up.

Marcia van Buskirk caught up with her as she headed toward the trailer to water Bunky. Like Jamie, she had dark hair and a slender build.

"Hey," her mother said.

"Hi," Jamie replied glumly. "Where did we lose all that time? That was bad."

Mrs. van Buskirk considered. "He looked pretty good overall, but he lost time on the second barrel. You really set him well on the first barrel, though, and hustled him good later." She patted Jamie's shoulder. "We'll get him next time."

Jamie smiled ruefully. "Yeah." Growing up with parents who rodeoed professionally, she'd always assumed she'd end up being like them. The thought that she might not eventually be good enough was too painful to think about.

Monday, Monday

The basement was dark and cold when the alarm went off. Jamie slapped at the clock until it stopped buzzing, then sat up with a groan.

Monday morning. School. Ugh.

She remained huddled under the warm covers for a minute, hoping the furnace would kick on. That was one major disadvantage to having a bedroom in the basement. Another was that the furnace, when it did kick on, sounded like a tornado ripping through the house. It made for some exciting moments in the middle of the night.

Her little brother and sister, Casey and Jodie, also had rooms in the basement. Jamie finally groaned and got up, scrambling into clothes as goosebumps prickled her skin. Her mom believed in the "every man for himself" method of child-raising, so if they didn't all get upstairs in time to make their own breakfasts and pack lunches before school, they'd do without.

Jamie rushed for the bathroom, but Casey beat her to it. She slapped the door in frustration and yelled, "Hurry up, Casey!" It was the same thing every morning.

Jamie glared at the door as her brother happily splashed water in the sink. "I bet the minute we all leave home Mom and Dad will build an extra bathroom and put a heater in the basement," she muttered.

She finally got her turn in the bathroom, then hastily ate breakfast and packed her lunch. "Let's go!" she yelled. "We're gonna be late!"

Casey and Jodie knew better than to lag behind. If they missed their ride with Jamie they'd have to walk from the ranch to school. They followed Jamie out to the "Pistachio," a green 1979 Pontiac Catalina. It was a huge, gas-guzzling monstrosity that could hold eight or ten people. Nobody else wanted to drive it. It took about an acre to turn around.

Jamie was tall for her age, but she still had to sit up straight to see over the dashboard. She had a full driver's license, since fifteen was the minimum age requirement in New Mexico.

Jamie dropped off her brother and sister at Raton Middle School and continued on toward the high school. If she didn't get there before the first bell she wouldn't have time to hang out with Beau or any of her other compadres.

Beau Chavez was her boyfriend, a defensive lineman on the Raton High School football team. He didn't understand her interest in rodeoing any more than she understood his interest in football, but somehow they stayed together. They'd been best friends since middle school.

Jamie smiled as she pointed the Pistachio toward the school, knowing that Beau would be waiting for her like always. She had already decided she wanted to marry him someday even though he wasn't a rodeo cowboy. In the small cattle ranching and coal mining town of Raton, there were a lot more cowboys than football players.

She was still smiling as she passed Mr. Heuschkel, the biology teacher, walking to school as always. Jamie wasn't in his class, but she always thought he walked like a scientist, with controlled, graceful movements. He was very tall and thin with a salt-and-pepper beard and wire-rim glasses. The word around school was that he was a brilliant teacher with a hard class.

Jamie and Beau.

Jamie parked and hurried inside, making a bee-line for the library where all her friends hung out before class. Beau was standing around talking to a couple of guys on the football team, but as soon as she walked in, he came over to meet her.

"Hi," she said breathlessly, clutching her lunch and a couple of books. "I didn't think I was going to make it on time today. Casey and Jodie were driving me crazy."

Beau gave her a lazy grin. The combination of dark hair, pale skin and clear blue eyes made him almost irresistible. "You don't *look* crazy," he said thoughtfully. "In fact, you look pretty good to me."

Jamie laughed. "You always say that no matter how bad I look!" She glanced around and saw an empty seat, an old velvet chair with a round back. "Come on, I'm going to grab that chair before somebody else does."

They chatted comfortably about their families, homework and after-school plans. "You going to City Market tonight?" Beau asked. City Market was a local grocery store with a large parking lot that had turned into a gathering place for the high schoolers. There wasn't much else to do in Raton.

"Can't," Jamie responded. "We give Bunky Mondays off, so I won't be working with him today, but I promised my dad I'd help move the cattle this afternoon."

Beau laughed. "I'd offer to come help, but the last time your dad asked me to help with the calves I almost passed out!"

That incident had become a favorite story at Jamie's house. The previous year, Jamie's father had suggested that her boyfriend might enjoy helping with the calves. Anxious to please him, fourteen-year-old Beau quickly agreed.

Frank van Buskirk was a five-time national and state bronc riding champion with skin deeply tanned from years working outdoors. He gave Beau a long, assessing look.

"My wife will show you how to leg out a calf so I can vaccinate it," he said. "It's a two-person job."

Marcia van Buskirk smiled encouragingly as she motioned Beau over. "It's easy once you get the hang of it.

Just step in behind the calf, like this—" she demonstrated "—then grab its hind leg and hold on while Frank flips it."

Her husband was already moving. With no apparent effort he reached under the calf and flipped it onto its side. Mrs. van Buskirk sank down with the calf until she was sitting on the ground behind it, still holding its hind leg.

Beau watched, not wanting to make a fool of himself when it was his turn. So far it looked pretty easy.

"Then you pull the top hind leg in toward your stomach," Mrs. van Buskirk said, "and put your foot up under the bottom hind leg to keep it pinned while Frank vaccinates it."

It only took her husband a moment to inject the squalling calf, then it was up and running away. Mrs. van Buskirk jumped up and dusted off her jeans. "See? Nothing to it."

"Yes, ma'am. I think I can do that."

Frank van Buskirk nodded briskly. "Okay. Why don't we start with that bull calf over there? Go ahead."

Beau squared his shoulders and approached the wary calf from behind. Before he could grab its leg, it sidled away from him. After several more comical attempts he finally dove in and grabbed its hind leg before it could move again.

"Got it," he said a little proudly. The calf was surprisingly calm now that he had its leg in a firm grip.

Once again, Mr. van Buskirk flipped the calf with no apparent effort. Beau didn't have to remember to slide down as the calf toppled; it pulled him down with it. He ended up with the squirming bull calf's hindquarters resting almost on his lap. He looked up, waiting for Mr. van Buskirk to inject the calf so he could let it go.

To his surprise, the rancher was holding a razor sharp pocket knife instead of a syringe. With a swiftness born of years of practice, Mr. van Buskirk castrated the calf with an efficient flash of the blade, then glanced over at Beau. The young football player's mouth was hanging open, the blood draining from his face. Mr. van Buskirk hid a smile as he finished vaccinating the bawling calf and motioned for Beau to release it.

"Have to castrate the bull calves unless we plan to breed them," he explained briefly. "Otherwise they get too hard to handle."

Beau closed his mouth and stood up on shaky legs. He'd never seen anything like that before, and he suspected Jamie's father had planned it that way on purpose. He took a deep breath and met the rancher's eyes squarely. "Which one's next?"

Mr. van Buskirk nodded toward a heifer and watched Beau stride toward it with determination. Jamie's boyfriend might not be a rodeo cowboy, but he wasn't a coward either.

A year later, Jamie still laughed when she thought about that scene. "I still can't believe my dad did that to you, but he's liked you ever since."

The two chatted comfortably until the bell rang. "Do you need to stop by your locker?" Beau asked. He always walked her to class at the beginning of the day and met her at her locker between classes. He knew her schedule as well as he did his own.

The school was laid out like a big U with a math and science wing, an English and business wing, and a library and home ec wing. As they left the library and walked through the science and math hallway, Jamie glanced idly into Mr. Heuschkel's classroom. The teacher was standing near his desk at the front of the room writing something on the blackboard. A strong smell of formaldehyde drifted into the hallway. It definitely smelled like a biology class!

Beau walked her to the doorway of her classroom, then waved and hurried off. As usual, she walked in with a big smile on her face.

Herding Birds

"Hey Lynnski, you're losing one!" shouted Frank van Buskirk.

Jamie quickly scanned the herd and spotted the straying cow. She cut it off before it could get far and edged it back into the herd with some difficulty. Her mom always said moving cattle was like trying to herd birds, but it was especially hard when it was a bunch of pregnant heifers with attitudes.

It was early January, and they were moving the herd to the calving pasture north of Clayton Highway, closer to the house so they could keep an eye on the cows and new calves as they arrived.

"Got it!" she called back.

Her dad usually called her Jamielynnski, or Lynnski for short. She understood where the "Lynn" part came from, since that was her middle name, but she was never sure how it had turned into "Lynnski."

She could see her mother on the other side of the herd, keeping the cattle moving. On a family ranch, everyone was expected to help out, and Jamie had been working the cattle for about as long as she could remember. There was no time for daydreaming when you were dealing with large animals that could weigh more than one thousand pounds. Disasters, or "wrecks" as they were known among cattlemen, could happen in the blink of an eye.

"If I holler 'stop', stop!" her mother had said at least a thousand times. "I'll explain later. In a wreck you've got to react instantly."

Jamie remembered vividly a wreck that had happened once when they were moving the cattle up to the mesa. One minute the steers were moving in an orderly bunch; the next they broke away and started running. They went thundering off in a panic across an uneven prairie filled with treacherous underbrush, rocks and deep prairie dog holes.

"A wreck is on!" her dad shouted, warning that a disaster was in progress.

Jamie responded instantly by riding flat out for the front of the herd to try to turn them. She knew without looking that her mom and dad were doing the same thing. They managed to stop the herd before any cows were injured and got them safely to the mesa.

Afterward, exhausted and dirty, they had returned to the house. Marcia patted Jamie's shoulder. "It about gave me a heart attack to see you laying on your horse's neck and flying across all those prairie dog holes like that. If you'd gone down we'd have had a bigger wreck than the cattle."

"Isn't that what you did?" Jamie asked curiously.

"Yes," Marcia admitted. "But I'm the mom."

Frank ran a large hand wearily across his face. "There's always something life-and-death happening on a farm. You have to focus on doing what's needed to correct the situation without wasting a lot time." He looked over at Jamie and added, "You did a good job out there, Lynnski, even if you did give your mother and me some new gray hairs."

Now, as the last of the herd shouldered their way peacefully through the gate into the calving pasture, Jamie was glad there'd been no more wrecks. She preferred to get her pulse-pounding excitement in the rodeo arena.

Jamie and her dad.

Of course, considering her recent barrel-racing outcome, maybe she performed better in real life where there was no invisible clock ticking in the background to distract her.

The basement was freezing as usual when Jamie went to bed that night. She burrowed under the covers and tried to fall asleep, but her mind continued to race. She replayed her last race, trying to figure out how to improve her time. She thought about how close they'd come that day to a wreck. She tried to remember if she had enough gas left in the Pistachio to get to school in the morning. She thought about Rosie the raccoon.

Finally she muttered, "I give up!" and irritably tossed aside the covers. Sleep just wasn't happening. She might as well read until she got drowsy.

She glanced at a couple of old magazines, then picked up a small red booklet with the snake and staff medical symbol on the front. It was the manual from the CPR class the rodeo team had been required to take eight or ten months before.

Jamie flipped through the pages looking at the pictures, then carried it back with her to bed. If a boring manual on cardiopulmonary resuscitation didn't put her to sleep, nothing would.

She began to read.

Rosie the Raccoon

Laughter rang out in the small school library before a sharp glance from the librarian quieted it down. Jamie and her friends were sharing funny stories as they waited for the first bell.

"So my dad convinced my mom that a baby raccoon would be a

Rosie chowing down on some Cheetos.

great pet," Jamie was saying. "He stole a kit out of a hollow tree down the road and brought it home for us, and we carried it around with us everywhere. Rosie even went to Texas with us when my dad was competing in the Mesquite Rodeo."

"In the car?" Nichole asked incredulously.

"Yep. It drove my mom crazy because every time we stopped, Rosie tried to follow us out. She almost got slammed in the door a million times." Jamie shook her head. "She was super cute when she was little. We had this baby bottle, and she'd lay back and suck on it till she fell asleep. She grew up to be a horrible monster, though. She got into everything. One time she poured flour all over the kitchen floor, then rolled around in it till she looked like a ghost raccoon. My mom finally said Rosie had to go live outside like other raccoons."

"So you threw her out?" Paige asked.

"Well, we tried to, but Rosie didn't want to go, so she was always breaking back into the house. She had hands like a monkey, so she could open doors. It got so we'd hear the doorknob rattle and everyone would yell, 'It's Rosie! Quick, lock the door!' If we didn't get there in time she'd walk right in. Then she'd bite us if we tried to pick her up and put her back outside."

Anjali was giggling. "So what'd you do?"

"My mom would lay a trail of Cheetos from wherever Rosie was through the living room, out the door and down the steps. Rosie really liked Cheetos. Then we'd all sort of watch while she ate her way along, then slam and lock the door behind her once she was outside." Jamie laughed. "She finally gave up and went to live with other raccoons, but when she had her first litter of kits, she tried to move them into the house! My mom about had a heart attack."

The bell interrupted, and the teenagers quickly dispersed. Beau walked Jamie to class and they talked about their plans that week. Jamie had another competition with the school rodeo team and Beau had a football practice. Life as usual.

Jamie got through her first class all right, but by second period her lack of sleep from the night before was causing her eyes to droop. She propped her chin on her hand and tried to keep from yawning. It was going to be a long day. She wished it was Friday instead of Tuesday.

After class, she walked slowly to her locker to get her algebra book for her next class. She made several unsuccessful attempts to get the lock open. She was still fumbling with it when Beau walked up.

"Need help with that?" he asked. He quickly rotated the dial and popped open the lock.

"Thanks," Jamie said, swinging open the locker to shove in one book and pull out another. "I couldn't sleep last night, so I'm moving slow today."

"Well you'd better speed up or you're going to be late to class. I need to run or I'll be late too. See you in a little while!"

Jamie sighed as Beau trotted off. The halls were already clearing as the other students disappeared into their classrooms. She was definitely going to be late. She started toward the science and math wing, hurrying but not quite motivated enough to run. By the time she approached the doorway to her classroom, the hall was completely empty.

Maybe it was the pungent scent of formaldehyde in the air, or maybe it was some other indefinable instinct that made her slow down and glance away from her own classroom at that moment—and straight into Mr. Heuschkel's room.

She stopped and stared. What was Mr. Heuschkel doing on the floor? He was lying face down on the brown-flecked linoleum in the narrow space between the desk and the blackboard, his arms to his sides. The bottoms of his shoes were toward her, his face turned toward the desk.

Is he looking for something under the desk? Jamie wondered, but a faint alarm was already sounding in the back of her mind. She took a hesitant step forward.

"Mr. Heuschkel?"

He didn't move. Jamie walked through the door and stopped again. "Mr. Heuschkel? Are you okay?"

By now she was close enough to see that his hands were palm up, his fingers curled in an unnatural position. He was completely still. Jamie stared at the back of his light-colored shirt, only gradually becoming aware that the normal rise and fall caused by breathing was absent. The faint alarm turned to an internal shriek.

Mr. Heuschkel was in trouble. There was no time to waste.

A wreck was on.

A Wreck Is On

Jamie quickly shook off her frozen state and forced herself to focus.

I can't reach him where he is, she thought, eyeing the narrow space between the desk and blackboard. I need to get him out.

Without hesitation, she bent down and grabbed the teacher's ankles, then leaned back and tugged. She worried briefly that she'd hurt him by dragging his face across the linoleum or catching his rigid fingers on one of the desk legs, but she dismissed the thought as silly. He looked dead, and nothing she could do could make that any worse.

Once she had him clear of the desk, she moved up beside him. His face was white and still, his eyes closed. Jamie was panting with exertion and fear. *Help me,* she prayed silently. *Show me what to do!*

The pages of the CPR manual she'd read the night before suddenly formed a clear picture in her mind: *The victim should be flat on his back on a level surface.*

I have to roll him over, she thought. She placed one hand on his shoulder nearest her and the other on his side, then lifted and pushed. The first time it didn't work; she lifted him partway, but wasn't prepared for the dead weight of someone his size. He flopped back down on his face. She immediately tried again, this time gritting her teeth and straining harder. With great difficulty she managed to roll him all the way onto his back.

She stared down at his face, seeing it clearly for the first time. His face was pale, his lips tinged with blue. He was totally still with none of the small movements that a sleeping or unconscious person makes. She knew then for sure that he wasn't alive.

Check for breathing and a heartbeat.

Jamie dragged her eyes away from his face and focused on what she needed to do. Almost automatically, she reached under his chin to tilt his head back and clear his airway, then lightly pressed two fingers to the side of his neck to check for a pulse. At the same time, she leaned down and put her ear close to his mouth so she could listen for breathing. His nose was ice cold against her cheek, like he'd just come in from outside.

If there's no breathing or pulse, start CPR.

Jamie felt like she was reading the manual, it was all so fresh in her mind. Keeping Mr. Heuschkel's head tilted back, she pinched his nose, drew in a deep breath, and bent down to seal her mouth over his.

Give two slow breaths, just until the chest rises.

She exhaled slowly, keeping one eye on Mr. Heuschkel's chest, just as she had practiced on the CPR mannequin. She was excited to see that it was working—his motionless chest slowly rose. She gave him a second slow breath, then quickly shifted her hands to his chest.

Find your hand position on the sternum.

Mr. Heuschkel was wearing a button-down shirt. Jamie swept her fingers along his rib cage to find the spot where his ribs met his breastbone, then used two fingers to measure up to where her hand should go. She planted the heel of her hand on his chest, then put her other hand on top of it so she could concentrate her weight on that one area. She positioned her shoulders over her hands and leaned her full weight into a sharp downward thrust with enough force to lift her off her knees.

Count aloud. Stay focused.

"*One* and *two* and *three* and *four* and *five!*" Jamie pumped Mr. Heuschkel's chest like a machine, determined to force life back into his body.

After the first round of heart compressions, she gave him two slow breaths, then moved back to his chest. She was sweeping her fingers along his ribs to find the right spot for her hands again when somebody came into the classroom and asked, "What's going on?"

She didn't even look up to see who it was. "Call 911!" she ordered. Hands in place, she started the next round of heart compressions.

"One and two and three and four . . . " Whoever it was turned and left in a rush.

Come on, Mr. Heuschkel, Jamie pleaded silently. Even if she had to pump his chest ten thousand times, she was determined that she'd get his heart going again.

With the next round of compressions she noticed where her hands were in relation to the buttons on the teacher's shirt. No sense in wasting time feeling his ribs each time if she could use the buttons as a marker.

Breaths, compressions. Breaths, compressions. Mr. Heuschkel remained lifeless.

With a clatter of heels, the home ec teacher ran in. "We've called an ambulance. What can I do to help you?"

Jamie glanced down at Mr. Heuschkel's white face. It wasn't in the CPR manual, but she remembered an old saying, "Face is red, raise the head, face is pale, raise the tail."

"Go ahead and raise his legs," she said breathlessly. Mrs. Poe immediately did as she asked.

After doing another round of heart compressions, though, Jamie realized that elevating Mr. Heuschkel's legs could make it harder to force his blood to circulate. The only thing moving blood and oxygen through his body was her determined pumping.

"Drop his legs," she said. Without hesitation, Mrs. Poe lowered them again.

Jamie was vaguely aware that other people were crowding into the room, but she kept her eyes on Mr. Heuschkel. She'd done about ten rounds of breaths and heart compressions when he suddenly opened his eyes and made a gurgling sound deep in his throat. She jerked her hands off his chest with a deep sense of relief. He was back!

"Mr. Heuschkel!" she exclaimed. "Mr. Heuschkel, can you hear me?"

To her dismay, his eyes slowly closed again. She felt frantically for a pulse. No matter how hard she tried, she couldn't feel the faintest beat beneath her fingers.

Tears welled in Jamie's eyes. Somehow this was a thousand times worse than walking in and finding him dead. He'd been alive again—just for a second, but alive!—and now this last little bit of life was fading out right in front of her. She was watching him die.

"No!" she said, both to herself and to Mr. Heuschkel. She started pumping his chest again.

A siren wailed outside as an ambulance pulled up, and a moment later the paramedics ran down the hall and into the classroom carrying their equipment. Jamie didn't look up. She remembered another instruction from her late night reading:

Continue CPR until emergency personnel arrive and tell you to step aside.

Until they told her to stop, she wasn't going to quit.

She was startled when, instead of telling her to step aside, one of the paramedics handed her a CPR mask to use—a plastic mask with a one-way air valve that fit over the victim's nose and mouth. It was designed to protect rescuers from any disease a victim might have. Jamie fit it over Mr. Heuschkel's face and bent down to give him breaths, but the angle of the mask made it hard for her to see if his chest was rising, the only way she could tell that her breaths were going in.

After several frustrating attempts to use the mask, Jamie tore it off and threw it across the room. "I can't use that thing!" she exclaimed. She went back to giving breaths as she'd done before.

The next few minutes passed in a blur as the paramedics attached wires to Mr. Heuschkel's chest and eventually loaded him onto a stretcher. As they rolled him out of the classroom, Jamie slowly stood up, feeling numb and breathless. Passing through the excited crowd of both students and teachers, she stumbled out into the hall and walked down to the library. She sank into the velvet cushion chair.

"Are you okay?" asked the librarian. "You look kind of pale."

Jamie stared at her, realizing that she had no idea what had just happened. "I'm fine. I just need to sit down for a minute."

The librarian smiled kindly, "Okay, but don't be late for your next class."

Jamie didn't care if she was late for her next class, but she was haunted by the thought that she might've been too late for poor Mr. Heuschkel.

Haunted

"Mom?" After tossing and turning for hours, Jamie had decided to go upstairs and talk to her mother. It was after midnight. Her father was already sound asleep.

Marcia van Buskirk put on a robe and followed her daughter out to the living room. She got comfortable on the couch, tucking her legs up under her, then looked at Jamie enquiringly.

"I can't sleep," Jamie said in a troubled voice.

"Because of what happened today?"

"Sort of." Jamie picked at the couch cushion. "What if Mr. Heuschkel lives, but he's brain damaged because I didn't do it right? He's so smart it would be especially hard for him."

Her mother looked at her steadily. "Honey, you did the best you could, and now the doctors are doing the best they can. They airlifted him to University Hospital in Albuquerque. Hopefully there'll be something in the paper in the morning to say how he's doing."

"I still can't sleep."

Mrs. van Buskirk eventually went back to bed. Jamie tiptoed back downstairs long enough to pull on sweats and a thick bathrobe, then slipped outside. She sat on the porch and hugged her knees to her chest, gazing into the night.

As her eyes grew accustomed to the darkness she noticed details—the dark outline of the mountains, the trees blowing in the wind, the big black shadow of the barn. The sky was crowded with stars, clear and bright at that high altitude. In the distance a coyote yipped. In the yard nearby, she heard the horses quietly moving around. There were a thousand small sounds she could pick out if she listened long enough.

There were few things more alive than a ranch.

Jamie pulled her robe closer against the chill. Life and death on a ranch were things she'd been raised to accept. Cute, brown-eyed calves were born too weak to suck and were lost. Horses fell onto sharp sticks or crashed in ditches and had to be shot. It was all heartbreaking, but nothing compared to watching Mr. Heuschkel's eyes slowly close after that brief flicker of life.

Jamie rested her forehead on her knees. Maybe I should've run out and called 911 before I tried doing CPR, she thought. I know he was getting my breaths, but I don't know if I was pressing his chest hard enough. If I'd called 911 first, the paramedics would've gotten there sooner.

She tried to remember how long a brain could go without oxygen before it was permanently damaged. Three minutes? Four? How long had it been before the ambulance got there?

Rodeos could be lost by the tick of a clock. So could human lives. What had she done?

She shivered and stood up. It was too cold to stay outside any longer. She spent hours pacing around her basement bedroom trying to relax, and finally slipped into a fitful slumber just before dawn.

The News

"Jamie? Mr. Heuschkel's going to be okay." Mrs. van Buskirk held up the newspaper as Jamie walked into the kitchen. Jamie snatched the paper and sat down to read it.

"It says his heart had some kind of an electrical malfunction," she said musingly when she finished the article. "Does that mean he'll have to get a pacemaker put in?"

Her mother shrugged. "I'm not really sure, but it says they expect him to recover and be back at work in a couple of weeks."

Jamie still had dark circles under her eyes, but she felt like a huge load had been lifted from her shoulders as she drove to school that day. She caught herself unconsciously watching for Mr. Heuschkel on the way to school, his long arms and legs swinging gracefully as he walked.

I'm probably delirious from lack of sleep, she thought.

She parked and ran inside, looking forward to getting back to normal. Instead, she was mobbed as soon as she stepped into the library.

"Hey Jame!" said Nichole. "How was it making out with Mr. Heuschkel?" She retreated, giggling, when Jamie turned to glare at her.

Another friend spoke up. "Too bad you didn't have a class with him. You'd have gotten an A for sure!"

It was clear that the news had rocketed through the school. It was also clear that her friends were never going to let her live it down. Beau and his jock buddies were the worst.

"I'm not sure I like my girl going around kissing other guys," Beau observed virtuously. "I'm shocked. Truly shocked."

His friend Brock stepped in. "Hey, Beau, leave her alone! She's a big hero now. I hear the school's planning to add a Jamie van Buskirk Day so we'll get an extra day off each year. Don't mess it up for the rest of us."

Danny and Garett, two other football players, dropped to their knees in front of her. "We're not worthy!" they chanted, bowing repeatedly to her.

Jamie's face was burning by the time the first bell rang. For the first time in as long as she could remember, she was glad it was time to go to class. Like the old saying went, no good deed goes unpunished!

A week or two later Jamie was on her way to algebra class when Mr. Heuschkel suddenly appeared in the hallway outside his classroom.

"Jamie?" he said. "Can I talk to you for a moment?"

"Sure," she replied awkwardly. It was the first time she'd seen him since he was dead. It made her feel kind of strange.

He appeared to be uncomfortable, too. "Well," he said, "I just wanted to come in and thank you for what you did. You saved my life."

Jamie shrugged self-consciously. "I'm glad you're okay. I was worried that I should've called an ambulance before I started doing CPR, but all I could think of was 'hurry, hurry!' You looked pretty bad."

"Then it's a good thing you followed your first instincts.

My doctors told me that if you'd left the room I would've died. You got to me just in time."

"Really?"

"Really." Mr. Heuschkel chuckled. "Of course, you broke a couple of my ribs when you were pounding on my chest, but that's okay."

Jamie gasped. "Oh no, I didn't really, did I? It's been awhile since I took the course, and I was afraid I wasn't pressing hard enough, so I kept putting all my weight into it. I just . . ."

"No, no, it's fine! Believe me, ribs mend a lot easier than hearts. You did everything just right." The teacher glanced around the hallway, then returned his gaze to Jamie. "I wouldn't be standing here today if you hadn't acted so quickly. I'll always be grateful for that."

"Oh. Well, I'd better get to class now."

Mr. Heuschkel nodded. "Stay in touch." By the time Jamie looked back he was gone.

And They Lived . . .

Beau Chavez and Jamie Lynn van Buskirk Chavez, newly married, happily moved among their wedding guests. After going steady all the way through high school, Beau had finally proposed. They were still best friends.

When the music started they danced together. Jamie felt a little strange wearing a satin wedding dress instead of her usual jeans, but she reminded herself that it wasn't every day you got married. Her mom and dad looked equally strange in their formal clothes. Beau looked as good in a tux as he did in a football uniform.

Jamie looked up to see Mr. Heuschkel walking toward her. He hadn't changed at all over the past few years.

"May I have this dance?" he asked politely.

She smiled and held out her hand.

Jamie and Mr. Heuschkel.

As Jamie suspected, as soon as she and her younger brother and sister left home, Mr. and Mrs. van Buskirk installed a nice, quiet wood-burning stove to heat the basement.

Would You Know How to Respond . . . Correctly in an Emergency?

Take this quiz and find out!

1. **Your body's involuntary response to a sudden, life-threatening situation will often include:**
   a. Calling 911
   b. Increasing the amount of adrenaline dumped into your system
   c. Increasing the blood flow to the large muscles of your arms and legs
   d. b and c

2. **This involuntary response puts you in "survival mode," commonly known as:**
   a. "Crocodile Rock"
   b. "Last Man Standing"
   c. "Weakest Link"
   d. "Fight or Flight"

3. **Your actions in an emergency will largely be determined by:**
   a. careful reasoning and decision-making on the spot
   b. whatever knowledge and skills you've already acquired
   c. what other people tell you to do
   d. your physical condition at the time

4. **Your ability to make good snap decisions in an emergency will usually be:**
   a. enhanced by the excitement of the moment
   b. about the same as at any other time
   c. impaired by the sudden change in your mental and physical state
   d. nonexistent; you're physically incapable of making snap decisions in an emergency

5. **If you're not in immediate danger, but are trying to help someone who is, the best plan is to:**
   a. "think on your feet", i.e. make up a plan as you go
   b. act on instinct
   c. take a few seconds to calm yourself so you can think clearly
   d. stop, look and listen

6. **The first goal in responding to any emergency is to:**
   a. take immediate action
   b. keep yourself alive and uninjured
   c. run away
   d. put on latex gloves and goggles

7. **The first rule in trying to help someone else in an emergency is:**
   a. do no further harm
   b. always carry your first aid certification card
   c. find out the person's name and next of kin
   d. wait for paramedics

8. **Seemingly harmless actions that can, in some instances, hurt ill or injured people include:**
   a. moving them
   b. giving them anything by mouth (i.e., food or water)
   c. giving them medicine (prescription or over the counter)
   d. all of the above

9. **In an real-life game of survival, which type of hero would score the lowest number of points?**
   a. Successful Hero (saves someone; survives uninjured)
   b. Unsuccessful Hero (fails in attempt to save someone; survives uninjured)
   c. Wannabe Hero (daydreams about rescue scenarios, plans how to react, takes training)
   d. Dead Hero (tries unsuccessfully to save someone; dies in the attempt)

10. **The best way to prepare yourself to respond correctly in an emergency is to:**
   a. watch reruns of *Rescue 911*
   b. take training courses from the Red Cross, Scout organizations or other recognized programs
   c. watch reruns of *ER*
   d. create real emergencies so you can practice handling them

Answers: 1-d, 2-d, 3-b, 4-c, 5-c, 6-b, 7-a, 8-d, 9-d, 10-b

Give yourself ten points for each correct answer, then check your score below:

90–100: *Teens 911 Top Gun.* You've demonstrated an unusually high level of knowledge and skills. Congratulations!

80: You've demonstrated an above-average level of knowledge and skills. Not bad.

60–70: While you've demonstrated at least some basic knowledge, it's not enough to keep you (or someone you're trying to help) out of trouble.

50 or Below: You know the Scouting motto about "being prepared"? Well, you're not! Better hope your friends and family are in better shape.

WANTED: TEEN HEROES AND SURVIVORS

Have you recently heard or read about a teenager who should be featured in a future volume of *Teens 911*? If so, send in a newspaper clipping or other information to help us track them down, and you might end up with *your* name in print!

We're looking for true stories involving teenagers who have used their knowledge and skills to dramatically save their own—or someone else's—life. If you're the first one to put us onto a story we're able to use, we'll print your name at the end of the story and send you a free, autographed copy of the book upon its release.

Send as many details as possible to:

TEENS 911
P.O. Box 461572
Garland, TX 75046-1572
E-mail: *books@realkids.com*
Web site: *www.realkids.com*

Be sure to include your name, address, phone number and e-mail address if you have one.